Hands-On Democracy

HOW YOU CAN TAKE PART IN CANADA'S RENEWAL

PATRICK BOYER

Copyright © 1993 by Patrick Boyer, MP

All rights reserved. No part of this publication may be reproduced or transmitted in any form or by any means, electronic or mechanical, including photocopying, recording, or any information storage and retrieval system, without permission in writing from the publisher.

First published in 1993 by
Stoddart Publishing Co. Limited
34 Lesmill Road
Toronto, Canada
M3B 2T6
(416) 445-3333

Cover Design: Brant Cowie/ArtPlus Limited
Author Photograph: Ron Watts

Printed and bound in Canada

Printed on paper
containing over 50%
recycled paper including
10% post-consumer fibre.

Contents

PREFACE *v*

CHAPTER ONE
IT'S TIME FOR RENEWAL *1*

CHAPTER TWO
LET'S CRUSH THE DEBT
(BEFORE IT CRUSHES US) *10*

CHAPTER THREE
CANADIAN PATRIOTISM
(THERE IS SUCH A THING) *35*

CHAPTER FOUR
WHAT CANADIANS WANT *53*

CHAPTER FIVE
LISTENING TO THE PEOPLE *63*

CHAPTER SIX
THE POLITICS OF ENGAGEMENT   *87*

CHAPTER SEVEN
DEMOCRATIC CONSERVATISM   *106*

ABOUT THE AUTHOR   *119*

Preface

We have entered a phase of history where fundamental changes are rapidly displacing the old order.

Accordingly, we are now faced with making major choices. It is not true that our future will "unfold as it should" if we are indifferent to it. Different roads are open to us, and while there is uncertainty about which is the best route to take, we are moving forward and therefore we must choose.

This book is my statement of a vision for Canada's future. It is about where we could go, and how, together in a new partnership, we can get there. As a small book it clearly does not contain a complete catalogue of all our choices, nor a detailed prescription for every last issue or problem we might encounter along the way, But you will find in it several major themes and a number of specific ideas about how we truly can move forward.

This book addresses the single theme of renewal. As a fiercely proud Canadian who dreams of how this country can yet become more than just the sum of its many parts, I set out my ideas for a new partnership in Canadian society, for a democracy that is truly engaging and vibrant.

From my experiences living and working in many parts of Canada I have gained an indelible belief in the strength and common sense of Canadian people. As a boy growing up in small-town Ontario, I came to understand public life and politics through the weekly newspaper that our family published, through the work my father performed as the elected representative to the Ontario Legislature, and through my late mother's contributions in church work and community service. As a university student in Ottawa, Montreal, and Toronto, I soaked up knowledge of our country and its ways. As a journalist in Saskatchewan, Ontario, and Quebec, I closely observed and described our people and their practices. As an author of nine books, I have clarified my thinking about aspects of our government and political system. As an assistant to opposition leader Robert Stanfield, as executive assistant to Ontario Attorney General Arthur Wishart, and as executive director of the Task Force on Conflict of Interest appointed by Prime Minister Pierre Trudeau, I witnessed the interaction of policy and politics at close range.

As Member of Parliament for Etobicoke-Lakeshore over the past nine years, chairing parliamentary committees and serving as a parliamentary secretary, I have rounded out further my experience and understanding of Canada's political institutions. At the core of this understanding remains my strong respect for the democratic instinct, and a confidence that we can, and must, govern with the trust of the people.

Over these same years, my observations about government, abuses in the exercise of power, excesses in some parts of our society, injustices and discrimination in others, human nature, and the need for accountability have contributed to a number of fundamental values which I hold.

I believe in the importance of each person, and that each person takes on his or her identity as a member of the community. I believe with passion that we are our brothers' and sisters' keepers, and share the joys and sorrows of our common humanity on this planet. I believe in individual self-reliance, the concept of duty and public service, and the importance of community. I recognize that traditions have value, that institutions help maintain order, and that patriotism is noble. I believe that the rule of law and maintenance of civil order are essential elements of a civilized society. I cherish and respect nature, and seek a holistic relationship that understands and accepts the primacy of our environment. I welcome a strong role for government, but do not believe that government can do everything; currently, government is trying to do too much. I am an integrationist, seeking to include all the parts and pieces into a coherent whole. I delight in the spiritual nature of our lives, and understand there are important realms for each of us that exist far beyond the call or command of any civil government.

At this time, when I am seeking to become leader of the Progressive Conservative Party and to become Prime Minister of Canada, this small book helps set out my approach both as a democrat and as a conservative. Even if I were not seeking a leadership role and high public office, I would want to say what is found in these pages because I believe in the timeliness and urgency of public debate and discussion about the future of our beloved country.

I believe there are essentially two kinds of leadership. The transactional leader seeks to broker the many interests that compete into a compromise, and the transaction or "deal" is the way this is done. The transformational leader seeks to inspire action within a new frame of reference, and is concerned more with values and vision than with the detailed workings of the existing system. I believe that Canadians are now ready to move forward, to address our future in new terms suited to our transforming world. This requires leadership that seeks a transformation — and that is what the new partnership and the program for renewal which I describe in the following pages is all about.

CHAPTER ONE

It's Time for Renewal

PRIME MINISTER BRIAN MULRONEY surprised many Canadians on February 24, 1993, when he announced that he would not fight a third election but would step aside to help create "a time of renewal."

All at once, the frame of reference for Canadians changed, and changed dramatically. The nature of our politics was suddenly transformed from mindless Mulroney-bashing to a deeper debate about exactly what "renewal" entails and what should be done about all the hard choices before us. The issue of our future became open again. The time had come to move forward. But in what direction, and with whom, and for what purposes?

This book is my attempt to answer those questions. The core of what I am advocating for renewal can be summed up in the phrase "hands-on democracy." This is a message about empowerment of individual Canadians, about reform of our political institutions, about an end to secrecy and apartness in government, and about a start to greater citizen involvement in decision-making.

Canadians have understandably distanced themselves from the top-down approach in government, the elitist or establishment-minded view those in power know best. The current mood in our country and the proposals in this book can, I believe, form the basis for a significant advancement of Canadian society into a far more integrated and holistic entity. We have already lived too long with our regionalism, parochialism, and fragmented image of ourselves. We are ready to create a new and broader sense of our Canadian community.

The world is changing dramatically. In the long view of our history as a country, I believe that the remaining years of this decade give us our best ever, and perhaps our final, opportunity to prove to ourselves and the world that a country of such diversity can in fact become more than just the sum of its parts. If Canada, a virtual United Nations within our own borders, can become truly unified and prosperous, then we will remain a shining example and inspiration for many other countries around the globe. That is why this time of renewal must not, for the sake of all that has gone before, be squandered.

This is not a time when building "more of the same" on existing foundations is adequate. The weariness of the old structure cannot be overcome simply with a new paint job.

We are in a time of "deconstruction" — by which I mean we are now engaged in dismantling an ideological edifice and all the structures and ideas that had become component parts of it, so that "reconstruction" can occur using those same parts according to a new blueprint.

For Canadians, like people in other countries where anger and disbelief have begun the deconstruction of the political mixture-as-before, life has not yet hit its new stride. It is clear that we are living in a new age, and not just because the Soviet Union has ceased to exist, or because surviving communist regimes appear much less threatening, or because communications technologies, fear of environmental degradation, and restructuring economies have all drastically altered the way we see and do things. It is clear this is a new epoch because "the old political litanies, even when used, are no longer believed," as Stephen Graubard observed in the fall of 1992. The shopworn rhetoric of the earlier era, even in its new formulations, "expresses nothing so much as social grievance and resentment, intellectual fatigue, cultural fear."

On October 26, 1992, Canadians came face to face with this transition. The "reality check" at the referendum ballot box on the constitutional proposals of the Charlottetown Accord showed that the people and the governments of Canada were not exactly in phase with one another. In that direct popular vote on proposals to fundamentally change our country's Constitution, the old approach was derailed and the political reconstruction of Canada begun.

We Canadians are changing our institutions, values, laws, and practices as we move from the old model of a nineteenth-century "nation-state" into a new model of a twenty-first-century "international country." Our evolving nature as a democratic society is taking place in this context of far-reaching economic, communications, and environmental change. The conflict between the political and cultural ideas of Canada as a nation is, at long last, being confronted.

Canadians seek to be released from shallow rhetoric that substitutes for policy, from forms that deaden life, and from rituals that produce conformity. The political imperative of our time is for new thinking, for a *coherent* approach to Canadian public policy, for a deconstruction of yesterday's orthodoxies, for a self-confident consideration and construction of the alternative.

As a democratic conservative, I see the uncertain days ahead containing both hope and opportunity. After all, this is not a phase of destruction of what now exists, but rather its deconstruction and subsequent reconstruction. We are not about to witness a "revolution" in Canada, but rather our "evolution" to a robust new stage.

ELEMENTS OF RENEWAL

Three fundamental transformations of the past decade set the context for the Mulroney government, and will continue to determine the direction of any government in Canada that succeeds it. The Cold War ended. The debt crisis accelerated. The sovereignty of the people emerged.

Old Ways Have Become a Casualty of Peace
First, the ending of the Cold War freed us from the long twilight struggle between communist and anti-communist forces, arrayed behind massive armaments and defence networks, distorting analysis and action at so many levels around the world. Canadian foreign policy and defence planning were constrained by this grim reality. Since the collapse of communism, much attention has naturally been focused on the countries of central and eastern Europe and their struggle to establish market economies and democratic political societies.

However, we ought to realize that just as the Cold War had two sides, its ending has equally affected our "side." Many people do not seem to have grasped how fundamental a change is afoot in the Western democracies, now thawed out from the Cold War. There is much more to this than simply spending the elusive "peace dividend" made possible by the step-down in military preparedness. The new frame of reference has dramatically altered political realities in the West as well.

Issues long suppressed, and spending priorities long established, have changed as a result of the end of the Cold War. We close our Canadian Armed Forces NATO bases in Germany, reduce the size of our Armed Forces in Canada, prepare to close surplus military bases, and question the usefulness of costly helicopters designed to hunt enemy submarines. More generally, we are finding a new freedom internationally to act according to long-standing Canadian interests, and need not any longer be so closely tied to the Americans or other members of "the Western Alliance" in our foreign policy. As a founding member of the United Nations, we see, finally, the chance for this global government to realize its real potential, and understand that a leadership role is ours in this new order. Within our country, too, the changed international context has produced a new awakening of interests and expectations.

Waking Up to the Icy Reality of Indebtedness
A second transforming event is the reality of our national debt. Talk of a "balanced budget" has long since receded into the mists of nostalgia. We are at this time so far removed from that objective that it is taunting the Canadian people even to speak of it — unless one is prepared to take truly bold measures. The crushing debt burden — where provinces run up annual operating deficits in the billions of dollars that only a few decades ago equalled the total Canadian national debt — has completely distorted the nature and operation of government in our country.

Efforts by the Mulroney government over the past few years to turn the tide on the debt have been significant. The annual operating deficit was turned into a healthy surplus. Tax loopholes were closed. Twenty-two crown corporations were sold off or wound up, and many government agencies and organizations, including such notable entities as the Law Reform

Commission of Canada and the Economic Council of Canada, were abolished. The size of the federal public service was shrunk back to its 1972 level, and wage freezes have been imposed across the board. Financial transfers to provincial governments were altered, and changes made — to programs from child benefits to unemployment insurance — reflecting this new fiscal reality.

Doing more with limited resources became the name of the game, for a while. For instance, the financial support for children in Canadian society was successfully revamped starting in January 1993 by concentrating the funds available on those most in need — lower-income working families. Yet the financial problems of governments at all levels in Canada today have now pushed us to the more drastic phase of having to do less, not more, with limited resources. We are in a time when realism, like a bucket of icy water, is dampening down expectations.

The weight of our cumulative national debt crushes down on governments, the private sector, and Canadian taxpayers alike. It slows our economic recovery. It reduces room for manoeuvring and limits the ability to respond to many issues and expectations still aroused in Canadian society. It is driving governments to slice here and cut there, like a surgeon trying to cure a patient's disease by a series of small amputations — a foot here, then a hand, next an ear. Yet even with all this pain and loss — invariably accompanied by demonstrations against government cutbacks, from VIA to UI, from pensions to the CBC — it has still not been enough. Our debt is so large that just paying the $40-billion interest on it every year means the government continues to operate with a large deficit, despite good financial management and all the pain of small amputations, from one department to another, from one program to the next.

It is as if we are still in the phoney war stage of dealing with our debt crisis. The new reality of Canadian politics is that the days of government spending are gone, and an era of radical restraint measures and fundamental reorganization of payment for social programs is at hand.

We simply cannot continue to watch tax-hungry governments continue their rampage in an endless quest for new sources of taxation and revenue. We saw perhaps the ultimate example of how bizarre government is becoming, driven insane by the quest to find more money, when the New Democratic government in Ontario (after Premier Bob Rae had previously condemned gambling as a tax on the poor, and after one of his cabinet ministers had written his Master's thesis on how casinos become magnets for crime) decided to set up gambling casinos in the province. At the same time, in the House of Commons, we were enacting legislation to abolish the six-month grace period following graduation for repayment of student loans, imposing a filing fee on lobbyists (although the government had three years earlier indicated this would not be done), and reducing cabinet ministers' salaries by 15%. Another ear. Another hand. Still sick.

A New Awareness of the Importance of Public Participation

The third transforming reality for Canadian politics came with the October 26, 1992, constitutional referendum. For several decades, major energies by Canadian governments had been directed to rewriting our existing Constitution. This enterprise became a costly burden for the country to bear. It consumed time, energy, money, but also distracted government and public policy-makers from a more forthright engagement of the Canadian people with Canada's major social, economic, and environmental agenda.

Major political issues, which in other countries would be dealt with in their congresses or parliaments, were here transferred from our legislatures to the alternate forum of "First Minister Federalism." The Prime Minister and the premiers, together with their officials, gathered and negotiated up and down, back and forth, endless variations of constitutional proposals. The process began to resemble a locomotive running forward on steel rails. It seemed unstoppable, and every time there was a constitutional failure, more cars were added to the train and more issues loaded on. The ultimate all-in load of the final "Canada round" — the Charlottetown Accord — came rumbling down the tracks in the autumn of 1992.

Not only was the constitutional locomotive derailed on October 26, with the direct vote of the people showing 55% of Canadians against, but in the process, many Canadians, by their participation in the referendum, came to realize and enjoy the new political liberation found in hands-on democracy.

Significantly, the combined political efforts of the Progressive Conservative, Liberal, and New Democratic parties and their campaign organizers, backed by extensive advertising, polling data, and media presentations, proved that no result could be extracted from the Canadian people at the ballot box that they were not willing to give. Not only did this put constitutional tinkering behind us, a blessing in itself, but it ushered in a healthy new awareness of the importance of full public participation in making fundamental decisions for our country.

A NEW PARTNERSHIP

The interaction of these three somewhat conflicting elements — the new freedom of thought and action in the post-Cold War era, the restraint on action and inability to respond due to the crushing public debt, and the awareness that a participatory democracy enables citizens to become more involved and responsible — presents us with new possibilities for a partnership in Canadian politics. The partnership draws together the need for those in government to govern and the need for the people to participate.

The new partnership will involve the people far more effectively in the process of deciding and implementing public policy. New methods of participation and shared decision-making are, in fact, the only possibility of coming to grips with the political and economic realities that will face any future Prime Minister, government, or political party in office.

As we plan how best to move forward, seeking the elements of renewal for Canada, we must concentrate on four fundamental areas that hold the key to a genuinely brighter Canadian future. These four are dealt with in the rest of this book. They are economic renewal (chapter two), the awakening of a new spirit of Canadian patriotism (chapter three), a new focus by the government of Canada on the personal security of individuals (chapter four), and a new agenda to create a hands-on democracy (chapters five, six, and seven).

CHAPTER TWO

Let's Crush the Debt (Before It Crushes Us)

W E BEGIN WITH ECONOMIC RENEWAL.

Many people talk about the economy as if it was a single entity, something one-dimensional, abstract, and remote. In fact the economy is made up of an endless series of transactions, large and small — from ships moving their cargoes in the Port of Vancouver or up the St. Lawrence Seaway, to the prairie farmer taking grain to market, the seamstress next door sewing a new dress, or the stockbroker downtown selling porkbelly futures. It's paying the barber, signing a contract to build a new house, or deciding whether to vacation in the United States or buy a new car. It's the government decision on the fate of the cod fishery in the North Atlantic, or on a change in the depreciation rates under the Tax Act. Our "economy" is an intricate web of millions of decisions made daily. Every Canadian is a player.

Because there are so many elements in the economy, not all of them are easily measured in the same way at the same time. Economists and statisticians have devised many measures of economic well-being — balance of payments, exchange rates, worker productivity, gross domestic product — which are cumulative expressions of how the economy is performing overall. Yet even many of these measurements do not accurately reflect the exciting expansion and dynamism which can occur in some parts of the economy while, simultaneously, other areas are faltering and failing. Traditional measurements, such as housing starts, automobile sales, or appliance purchases, hardly record the current growth and vitality of the Canadian computer and telecommunication industries. As we have moved more into a service-oriented and information-based economy, the traditional way of looking at economic performance is sometimes unnecessarily depressing. The fact is the Canadian economy today is extremely dynamic and diverse.

Our economic well-being is the basis for the prosperity needed to support the services and social programs that have become a civilizing hallmark of Canadian life. Our education programs, our health care, our community and social services and so much more are all provided by governments and depend on economic strength to sustain them.

In my view, renewal of the Canadian economy as we move forward through the decade of the 1990s will require less government intervention, not more. The discipline and operation of market forces, and greater reliance on the private sector rather than the public sector, will be an important pathway to prosperity. We have already seen under the Mulroney government significant advances toward deregulation, privatization, and elimination of government red tape from business activity.

In moving forward now, I believe three dimensions of economic activity require particular focus by the government of Canada because they are the keys to our economic renewal: maintaining open markets, addressing the debt crisis, and upgrading workers' skills and freeing Canadian workers for greater productivity through new attitudes of participation and front-line responsibility.

OPEN MARKETS —
TRADING OUR WAY TO PROSPERITY

By "open markets" I mean the important role of unrestricted trade, the free movement of goods, services, people, and capital.

Trade between nations is the basis of prosperity, and the greatest guarantee of peace among nations. Countries that are major trading partners seldom go to war against each other.

Our economic renewal can be based on trading our way to prosperity. Canada's strength historically has been as a trading nation, and we have evolved from early trade in timber and furs to our highly manufactured and value-added products of the 1990s. In 1993, the recovery from the recession has been led by a dramatic increase in Canadian exports of goods and services, principally to the United States, helped by the Free Trade Agreement. Our foreign trade surplus is running strong, at an historical high.

Three strategies will help us maintain open markets.

First, we must continue progress to eliminate interprovincial trade barriers within Canada. It has been ludicrous, at a time of opening up better trading opportunities with other countries, that we have continued to have several hundred barriers to trade within our own country. A 1991 study by the Canadian Manufacturers Association, which estimated at 500 the number of trade-strangling provincial policies, figured their cost to our economy each year hits $6.5-billion. The Conference Board of Canada reported in 1992 that trade in certain goods and services is already freer between Canada and the United States than between Canadian provinces. The current plan to eliminate these barriers by June 30, 1994, must be vigorously pursued and concluded on that timetable, if not sooner.

Second, we must continue and enhance our trade arrangements in the North American hemisphere, under the Free

Trade Agreement with the USA, and now the North American Free Trade Agreement with that country and Mexico. Because a recession hit Canada just as the former trade treaty began to be implemented, many people have understandably blamed free trade as the cause of so much economic woe. In truth, the recession itself and economic restructuring due to global organization and automation have accounted for most job losses in the Canadian economy, while the trade treaty can be credited with just as much success in helping us out of the recession as it can be blamed for causing our recent difficulties.

Certainly our position next door to the United States, the world's most affluent and dynamic marketplace, puts us at the envy of virtually every other country in the world. The opportunity for Canadians is golden, and the trade treaties with the United States and Mexico, by further opening their markets to us, present great opportunities for future prosperity, if we have the competitiveness and self-confidence to take advantage of our unique situation. The good news is that this is only the beginning. Other countries in Central and South America also wish to join our dynamic trading block, and at last we will gain a secure basis for prosperity through trade.

Third, we must develop our relationship with all other major trading countries of the world, those who, like us, are members of the General Agreement on Tariffs and Trade (GATT). For some time now negotiations have been going on in the long series of GATT discussions by which further tariffs are to be reduced and trade opportunities expanded. This most recent phase of GATT discussions, known as the Uruguay round, raises the prospects of a vastly improved financial situation for Canada if the issues relating to agricultural subsidies can be resolved.

Most countries subsidize their farmers, and the result is that taxpayers are putting a lot of money into farmers' pockets through government funding programs, rather than spending their money at the grocery store for higher-priced but unsubsidized food products. The network of subsidies, quotas, and price regulation through marketing boards has grown to be a monumental cost to Canadians, both as taxpayers and, for some products, as consumers. When the governments of the big countries of the world compete by heavily subsidizing their farmers, such as the Americans and the Europeans do, it creates a financially impossible position for smaller countries like Canada.

Hard issues await resolution in trade negotiations that will put a cease-fire to the trade wars in agricultural produce between large countries whose farmers are heavily subsidized. In this process we may get back to a more open market and a freer interaction of supply and demand in agricultural products that could see the elimination of marketing boards and quota systems in Canada. This adjustment would be bitterly resisted by those who have benefited from the present highly regulated agricultural markets, but Canadian consumers, taxpayers, and ultimately farmers would benefit in the long run.

CRUSHING THE DEBT

Yet even success with these trade strategies for open markets could see our economy founder on the shoals of another stark reality: our national debt.

Canada has gotten itself into a desperate crisis of indebtedness. Our public and foreign debts — now around $615-billion and $300-billion respectively — have become so great that their combined weight is crushing down on government, the private sector, and individual taxpayers.

Canada is probably about ten years ahead of the U.S. and close to Italy in the supercycle/debt trap, suggests the *Bank*

Credit Analyst in *Outlook 1993*. Indeed, because of our much higher foreign debt, we are arguably even worse off than Italy and are, suggests the *Analyst*, "much closer to many Latin American countries in the 1980s."

Here's the prognosis in *Outlook 1993*: "A full-fledged crisis is brewing and policy is adrift because politicians at all levels have no idea what to do. They are paralysed. Leadership is weak, directionless, and without vision or principle. Therefore, you cannot expect an early resolution to the critical problems. Unfortunately, Canadians are still hanging onto the free lunch/sheltered workshop environment, and they keep electing politicians who promise more of the same. Until there is a clean slate of politicians in Ottawa and the provinces with a mandate to change course, you must prepare for the inevitable financial and economic train wreck."

The total government debt to gross domestic product ratio has climbed dramatically in the past twenty years, from around 40% to 90%. The fiscal deficit of the government of Canada, around $35-billion annually, consumes 5% of GDP. Taking into account the deficits of the provincial governments, the total rises to $60-billion, or 8.5% of GDP. These are record high deficit and debt levels. They are made worse by the fact that about 40% of Canada's debt is held by foreigners who are becoming less interested in buying Canadian debt. When we pay the interest on that foreign debt, it is hard currency leaving our economy.

How serious is this getting? In the month of January 1993 alone, Canada sold a record $6-billion in securities to foreigners, in spite of the growing concern that a national debt crisis is upon us. Foreigners bought those securities only because Canada is paying an ever-increasing interest rate, noted Greg Ip of *The Financial Post*. January's net investment by foreigners broke the previous record of $5.8-billion in October 1991. It followed a strong $3.6-billion investment in December, and is triple the $2-billion monthly average for 1992.

Foreigners, as a result, hold an increasing claim on Canadian income, representing the interest on Canada's foreign debt. As the size of off-shore borrowing hits record new highs, and the interest rates we have to pay to get this money keep climbing, it is clear how the heavy weight of debt on all levels of government is rapidly diminishing our prospects and our room to manoeuvre.

Even the Governor of the Bank of Canada, John Crow, stressed, in his annual report in March 1993, the sad state of public finance and noted how the debt build-up has reduced the capacity of governments to ease the harsh effects of the recession.

Major Canadian policy organizations have been going public with highly critical analyses about Canada's drift into indebtedness and the pending crisis. In February 1993 the C.D. Howe Institute, for example, released a sombre message that Canada is fast approaching a crisis point, where continued heavy borrowing may not be possible. A slow economy, low inflation, and high real interest rates were seen as factors working against deficit reduction. Moreover, the debt problem's low position on the public and political agenda prompted considerable pessimism about whether it would be addressed in time.

One of the institute's clear messages: *Fiscal retrenchment forced by an abrupt end to investors' willingness to buy Canadian debt would be far more damaging to Canadians' living standards than would a timely, controlled budget balancing process.*

Another Canadian think tank, the Fraser Institute, has been a consistent voice, years ahead of its time as far as public acceptance has been concerned, in pointing out how Canadians face a serious threat from the fiscal deficits incurred by our governments. Since at least 1976, when the institute proposed creation of a Government Expenditure Review Board to enforce tough spending controls, Michael Walker and others at the institute have issued many books and studies containing corrective proposals for the debt crisis.

This year, 1993, the institute is issuing three separate studies with specific solutions for the deficit problem. All of their solutions relate to spending control; there are no suggestions for increased taxes. The first study outlines structural changes in the current programs operated by the government of Canada. The second pertains to some 1,500 specific ideas that can generate significant savings, mostly for the federal government. The third group of solutions will address the activities of the provincial governments.

As the Fraser Institute notes, reduction of the deficit must involve reduction in actual program spending. Because the cost of government operations is 13% of the total Canadian budget, while the interest payments on the debt take up a much larger 25%, even a complete elimination of the entire Canadian government apparatus would not eliminate the deficit. On the other hand, even moderate percentage cuts in program spending would have a significant impact on spending and hence on the deficit, for the simple reason that payments to individuals account for 27% of the budget, while other program spending makes up the even higher remaining portion of 34%.

Cutting program spending means either paying fewer benefits to those who receive them, or paying benefits to fewer people. The Fraser Institute and others have suggested effective ways to cut spending by the Canadian government, particularly in the realm of transfer payments.

There is still great scope for spending reduction in the Canadian budget that has not yet been used, but it will involve the willingness to adopt a set of principles regarding who will receive social welfare payments, together with a concept of "income adequacy" that involves recognizing the family unit as the appropriate focus. These principles have already been implemented by the Mulroney government in changes to unemployment insurance, old age pensions, and the family allowance. The continuing dilemma of the government's finances suggests the time is at hand to apply these same principles to yet more programs, and indeed it can be done positively in a way that will help people break out of the welfare cycle of dependency.

The C.D. Howe Institute and the Fraser Institute are not the only voices addressing the financial plight of the country. Similarly, Burns Fry economists Dr. Sherry Cooper and Ted Carmichael met in the early months of 1993 with government of Canada and provincial government policy-makers and Canadian business leaders to explain their analysis of Canada's looming debt crisis. They stressed that Canada may soon need an International Monetary Fund bailout, as have other Western industrial democracies recently (more on this below).

In response to this growing crisis of indebtedness, Finance Minister Michael Wilson and subsequently Finance Minister Don Mazankowski have battled hard and made significant steps to bring the situation under control. No Canadian could have escaped hearing the howls of protest that greeted their budgets!

Canada Post and VIA Rail were put on a sounder business basis of operation with less taxpayer subsidization. Public servants went on strike, you may recall, in opposition to the government's wage-freeze policy. Criticism rang throughout the land and from the opposition parties in Parliament as crown corporations were sold off, tax loopholes closed, and the size of the Canadian public service reduced to its 1972 level. Several rounds of significant budget reductions for all government departments produced pain and outcry everywhere the axe fell. Some Canadian embassies overseas were closed, the Economic Council of Canada discontinued, the Law Reform Commission of Canada abolished, the Canadian Wildlife Service decimated, and the rate of increase of transfer payments to the provinces reduced. The list of hard decisions is already long. As painful and controversial as all this was, these now seem to have been the easy steps.

The Mulroney government succeeded in wiping out the red ink with which the Liberals used to write the annual budget for the country, so that on current account the government of Canada for several years now has been running an operating surplus. Yet the nightmare reality endures: a massive $40-billion each year must still be paid on the interest of our national debt. This does not reduce the debt, it just covers the carrying charges, the interest payments. Canada is *borrowing money to pay interest on the debt.* This amount of interest payment alone more than wipes out the operating surplus, so we continue to have deficits in the $30- to $35-billion range each year. This in turn means the cumulative national debt keeps growing. This is the supercycle debt trap. We just keep digging ourselves into a deeper hole.

The situation in most provinces has been the same, in many much worse. Once-mighty Ontario has become a pathetic example of gross indebtedness, with Ontario Hydro alone carrying a $34-billion debt and the province's budget for this current year showing a $13-billion deficit. It all gets added to Ontario's total provincial debt, which now has climbed to $65-billion. Quite predictably, financial markets have responded: Ontario's credit rating has been downgraded. In short, as Ontario borrows ever more money to cover its debts, it has to pay even higher interest rates for that money because of its diminished credit rating and ever-bleaker financial picture.

Let's Crush the Debt (Before It Crushes Us)

When you take into account the cumulative debt of the government of Canada and provincial governments, the staggering amount of $615-billion, you glimpse the ugly portrait of a crisis. It means a $23,000 debt for each Canadian. That compares with a per capita indebtedness of $14,500 for each American — and Americans are in deep turmoil about their debt crisis, with strong popular support even for President Clinton's recently proposed tax increases.

We are going to have to take a deep breath and take some strong medicine: *We must declare a moratorium on government spending.*

Many projects are justifiable on their own terms, but are not affordable when viewed in the larger context of our debt crisis. Many Canadians have come to expect governments to take care of their needs, to "be there" for them. This expectation is found not only among individuals, but also in organizations and businesses. Yet we can no longer keep borrowing money to pay for things we do not need or cannot afford.

There is no more room in the Canadian system for tax increases to cover the indebtedness, either. While some slight adjustments may be required in certain taxes, the broad picture is clear: *Further tax increases will not help us solve this dilemma.*

In fact our present tax levels have already become counter-productive. Just look at the falling tax revenues of governments in Canada this past year. While some of this shortfall is due to the recession, there are two other contributing factors. The underground economy has grown dramatically, simply because many people have chosen to buy goods and provide services for cash transactions which are never recorded, as a means for avoiding taxation. Second, many Canadians and their money are simply leaving for other countries with lower taxes. A flight of capital invariably is part of the pattern of true crisis, as history has shown us, from such countries as Argentina earlier in this century to Italy in recent months.

The only way to respond to the debt crisis is through a dramatic break with past and present practices of government spending, to accelerate budget restriction measures of Finance Ministers Wilson and Mazankowski, and to give Canadians clear talk and hard information on this crisis so they can lower their expectations of what government can or ought to do. The prevailing sentiment over the past several decades has people expecting government to be able to provide financial assistance, to be the "safety net," to guarantee the loan or spend money on each proposal and every program. For many Canadians expectations remain unrealistically high. The crisis of the debt is not even showing up yet on their radar screens.

Some Canadians have falsely assumed that the debt didn't matter, that we could keep having all our existing programs and services from government. If there wasn't enough money to pay for them, we could simply borrow to cover the shortfall. So borrow we did — some $60-billion last year. It seemed, for a while, that we could have the world's best welfare state — for individuals and corporations alike — without worrying about the economy. Yet 40% of our debt is now held by foreigners, and as stated above, they are rapidly losing interest in continuing to buy our government bonds. What happens when we can no longer keep borrowing, when we can't continue living on the credit of tomorrow?

It's at this point that the International Monetary Fund could enter the picture. If a financial crisis hits, the IMF might be needed to help resolve the situation. In that case, it would seek strict terms and conditions on cuts in the government deficit needed to put Canada's financial house in order. Perhaps some Canadians think this could not happen here. We are after all an important industrial democracy of the Western world. Yet consider this:

- In 1976 the IMF was called in by the United Kingdom and set out the terms for an austerity program to cut the budget deficit by 4% of GDP in two years.
- In 1974 through to 1978, the IMF was in Italy directing an austerity program to help the sick Italian economy and returned to that country in 1992 with another such program, following the collapse of Italy's long-term bond market and a flight of capital. Italy adopted a program to cut its deficit by 6% of GDP, and spending cuts included health benefits and pensions.
- In 1982 Ireland was forced to adopt an austerity program to bring its government debt under control.
- In 1992, Sweden's deficit problem contributed to a currency crisis. All parties in Sweden endorsed deficit cuts of 4% of GDP over two years including reductions in child benefits, housing subsidies, pensions, disability benefits, and foreign aid.
- And consider some other notable countries in the world, such as Argentina and Uruguay. Earlier in this century they had very advanced economies and significant government programs for the benefit of their people. Yet a loss of internal confidence, a flight of capital, and an economic collapse saw these countries fall, never again to fully recover their former prominence.

If the current trends in Canada continue, it is not far fetched to anticipate the IMF taking a hand in Canadian policy decisions. As a Canadian I would profoundly lament such a day. It would mean a loss of our sovereignty. It would be an admission to the world that we were not truly a self-governing people. It would also mean that many programs and values important to us as Canadians would be jeopardized in the dramatic restructuring that a fiscal crisis would necessitate. Those who have recently written to me protesting the government's 10% budget cuts as they affected their own programs would, I suppose, redirect their letters to the IMF bemoaning a cut of 60%.

Even if the IMF would not formally become involved in setting conditions for Canada, the same process is already under way, being dealt with by the credit rating agencies (which have recently been downgrading the credit standing of several provinces) and by the international financial community. Others beyond our borders make decisions in relation to our debt crisis that have a direct impact on us and our long-term prospects.

By taking the tough steps ourselves, we can with more care preserve values and approaches that are important to us as Canadians. Although we are dealing with harsh economic realities, at the end of the day the dilemma will, at least to some extent, be resolved by the operation of political forces and through the making of political decisions.

We must, I believe, take six steps to resolve the debt crisis.

Step 1: Declare a Moratorium on Government Spending

The government of Canada simply must stop spending money it does not have. This applies to everything from multi-billion-dollar procurement contracts (such as for the submarine hunting EH-101 helicopters for the frigates) to the smallest purchase orders. *The government will have to make do with what it has or go without.*

Government spending in big projects, like participation in the Hibernia oil consortium, must also come within this uncompromising approach of ending the spending. If the Hibernia project is worth doing according to market forces, then the private sector oil companies can do it and Canadian taxpayers need not be a subsidizing party to this enterprise. These are the real-world, specific examples, and there are many more — right across the board.

The spending moratorium should apply for thirty-six months.

Step 2: Case by Case — Postpone, Reduce, or Eliminate

The Parliamentary Committee on Finance should be given an immediate mandate to conduct an across-the-board review of all spending programs and recommend which can be postponed, which reduced, and which cancelled altogether.

The committee ought to use the same stern standards the IMF would in the circumstances, but pay greater attention to the political values and social fabric of Canada in doing so, more than an outside economist or banker would.

Step 3: Develop a Comprehensive All-Governments Budget

A common Canadian budget should be developed by all levels of government, and then strictly adhered to. Each government must agree to limit borrowing, to limit taxation, and then to sustain further spending cuts. Yes, this is radical, nothing short of a joint budgeting exercise by the government of Canada and provincial governments (and through them the municipalities) so that overall spending and borrowing can be controlled.

Agreeing to limit taxes overall is important, because when the government of Canada in a recent budget lowered taxes, provincial governments in Ontario and B.C. raised their taxes to recapture the amount, and then some. This is self-defeating.

Another reason for developing a common Canadian budget is that there has simply been too much blame-passing from one government to another in this country. The imperative of responding to the debt crisis has reduced the ideological differences between political parties in office and has given rise to a "common cause" such as one normally finds in the face of an external threat, such as during wartime. Even the New Democratic government in Ontario, after initially seeking to end the recession by stimulating the economy through spending and giving large pay increases to the public servants of the province, realized that this classic approach of Keynesian economics (still propagated today by John Kenneth Galbraith) no longer works when governments are so short of money that they are borrowing from abroad just to pay the interest on the debt. After trial and error, Ontario's government accepted that cuts in government spending are essential in coming to grips with the debt crisis, that a roll-back in public service salaries is required, and that the debt crisis itself is one of the contributing factors to our inability to emerge robustly from the recession.

The same approach, now taken by the NDP government in Saskatchewan, and Liberal governments in New Brunswick and Newfoundland, points to the greater likelihood of cooperation, in face of economic danger, in developing a coherent approach to government budgeting.

Step 4: Unilateral Action by the Government of Canada If Needed

Failure to gain the cooperation of the provinces could lead to other action by Ottawa to resolve the debt situation. Just as in wartime or other national emergencies, the government of Canada may assert its constitutional authority to resolve the debt crisis unilaterally.

In 1976 we saw the Supreme Court of Canada uphold Ottawa's power to impose price and wage controls even in the face of opposition by several provinces. We need a government of Canada that will govern for Canada. Better that than an unwelcomed visit by the International Monetary Fund.

Step 5: End the Transfer Payments

A complex formula exists for the Canadian government to transfer money to qualifying provinces. It's a way of spreading the money around the country, so that less-prosperous regions or provinces are a little more equal to the financially stronger provinces.

These equalization payments emerged from an earlier time in Canadian history, a product of the Depression of the 1930s when Alberta and Saskatchewan essentially became bankrupt. The government of Canada not only stepped in at the time, but also established the Rowell-Sirois Commission, which recommended a permanent system of transfer payments.

Over the decades since then, the administrative structure within the Canadian federal system to accommodate the transfers has become just one more element of unrealism in creating the attitude that even when a government didn't have the money it needed, it could somehow get it as of right. For a long time this approach was justified in political as well as economic terms, on the grounds that especially "fat cat" Ontario put up a very large share of the money that the government of Canada transferred. That gave a special sense of justice and satisfaction to many Canadians. Even back in 1967, Ontario Premier John Robarts looked at transfer payments and warned, "Don't kill the goose that lays the golden eggs." Today, Ontario is not producing many golden eggs, and the goose herself is being cooked. The political and economic climate are changing, and so is the context for Ottawa administered equalization payments and transfer programs.

When a country reaches the position of indebtedness we find ourselves in, there are no sacred cows left, let alone "sacred trusts." All of these programs involving transfer payments and the system of shared-cost programs must be revisited and revamped, for the dual objective of saving money and introducing cost controls.

Under our new (since the October 26 referendum) strict approach to living within the existing Constitution, we will increasingly revert to an old principle: *Ottawa and the provinces should each raise their own revenues to spend within their own jurisdictions.* We will fall back more and more on classic federalism: *sovereign governments exercising sovereignty in their own spheres.* This clarity will also help in laying the basis for a common Canadian budget approach while we work our way out of the debt crisis.

The debt mess will only worsen if all the provinces remain convinced that Ottawa won't let them fail. Apart from being a good way to avoid costly duplication, being more careful about not spending in another government's jurisdiction seems all the more important in keeping the lines clear if Ottawa is in some cases eventually going to have to bail out bankrupt provinces.

Step 6: Introduce User Fees for Moderation and Cost-Control
We have developed a broad range of social programs that make Canada a unique place in which to live. The challenge now is to find the way to keep these programs working for Canadians as we're running out of money to pay for them. This debate is not about whether to have social programs, but rather how to ensure they are sustainable.

Most of us, for example, are extremely proud of our health care system. We smile smugly when told that the Americans spend even more on health care than we do — and that, nevertheless, some 40-million U.S. citizens remain uncovered by basic medical insurance. We're proud that the new American president Bill Clinton is looking north of the border for ideas to improve his country's medicare system.

It is true that in major respects we compare favourably to the USA on this score. Yet the world is larger than that. If we contrast the Canadian situation with that of the major European countries, for instance, we would see that we are spending more on health-care costs than they, but doing less well when measured by the results of a health-care system (morbidity rates and the like).

Even on our own terms, up to 40% of the budgets of some provinces are consumed by health costs alone. The system is substantially funded by the government of Canada, but not really controlled by it, since the money passes through to provincial governments. The provincial governments in turn do not particularly regulate or control the health-care system. What we have is, after all, state-operated medical insurance to pay the costs of a private health-care system delivered through hospitals and by doctors, not a system of state-run medicine. Often the efforts at control (such as the prohibition of extra-billing by medical doctors) is ineffectually enforced by government, as doctors go unchallenged when levying an "administrative fee" on their patients to replace the prohibited extra billing.

The central issue here, in terms of government debt, is that many people believe they are receiving free medical care. Yet just because one can go into a doctor's office or be admitted to a hospital without having to pay upon leaving does not mean that this service is free. In this current year we taxpayers are footing a whopping $46-billion to pay our collective medical bills.

This financial dilemma cries out for resolution. A number of solutions are being implemented (from closing of hospital beds to creating a community-based health-care system that depends less on costly institutions) while other solutions are at the stage of being considered, from fixed salaries for medical doctors to user fees for patients. Many other solutions are currently proposed. The goal in all of this, of course, is to maintain a quality system of health care, without the country going broke in the process. My goal is to keep a health-care system we are proud of.

At present the government of Canada opposes user fees, although several provincial governments now appear closer to recognizing this as one part of the overall solution. In French an expression for "user fee" is "ticket modérateur," an interesting translation since the word *modérateur* suggests a moderating influence. Sometimes the phrase is used in English as "deterrent fee," which certainly puts a harder edge on the point being made. Whatever you call it, even a modest charge for each use of medical services would help greatly to cover the costs and reduce abuse.

It's a curious fact of human nature to believe that if something is paid for by the taxpayers, it somehow is free. I was recently stopped by a constituent who complained that since our party had been in office the price of a postage stamp had risen from 32 to 43 cents. "That is true," I explained, "but you are only paying for the stamp once, not twice."

"What do you mean?" he asked, looking somewhat bewildered.

"You used to pay for your stamp once when you bought it at the wicket at the post office," I said, "and then a second time when you sent in your income-tax return."

That's not happening anymore, because Canada Post is no longer being subsidized by the taxpayers. In fact it has been operating at a profit recently, and paying a dividend back to the government.

These six steps constitute radical surgery. The surgery will hurt. Yet consider the alternative: the painful destruction of Canadian life as we know it through the ravaging disease of debt.

Upgrading Workers' Skills and Fostering an Entrepreneurial Democracy

Chances are you have already done many things today that you couldn't five years ago, all because of changes in technology.

Instead of speaking with the receptionist or secretary when you telephoned someone's office, you probably left a voice mail message.

Or perhaps you have just picked up some flyers from the local printer, printed in record time, and without the services of a typesetter, because the computer produced camera-ready copy for the press.

What about the series of television documentaries you have been following for a school essay or a professional research project? Have they been conveniently recorded by your VCR while you went about other business?

Or the urgent document you used to send by courier has just been instantly transmitted across town, or around the globe, by fax.

Ours age is rapidly eliminating jobs through technology, and changing our patterns of behaviour in the process. Our service-oriented society, and our information-based economy, have required those who wish to have gainful employment to see life as one long program of continuing adult education.

In my constituency of Etobicoke-Lakeshore a motor oil company changed production and packaging methods three times in a decade. The metal cans for the motor oil were replaced by aluminum-lined cardboard containers, and a few years later these were replaced by plastic bottles. With this last change came introduction of computerized equipment into the plant, and the workers were all given courses to upgrade their skills. Many had not been near a classroom for years, some having finished their education only partway through high school. Management was apprehensive about the change, fearing that the workers would shy away from the advanced mysteries of the new world of computers. In fact only two men in the entire workforce found they could not cope with learning about computers, and were given alternate work to do. All the others, who had considered themselves in essentially a dead-end job in an assembly-line plant, awakened to the excitement of learning new skills and seeing how they could apply them with spectacular results in their workplace. The mood in the plant became transformed, as well, as these workers with their new skills gained for themselves a new measure of self-respect and freedom.

The key to economic renewal for Canada is the continuous effort to ensure that each Canadian who wants to work has the opportunity to acquire new skills, and is encouraged to do so. It is at this individual level that we can spark our economic renewal through increasing productivity — more accomplished at the end of the day using the same amount of resources.

Technical training has for years been an important part of Canada's education system. Technical schools and community colleges have helped many younger Canadians onto a productive pathway for their careers. The accelerating pace of automation and technical innovation means, however, that in virtually every trade or occupation, refresher courses are the key to staying abreast of change and remaining competitive.

In Prince Edward Island, a community college has come up with the innovative concept of a "warranty" that goes with each graduate. For instance, when someone graduating in computer technology lands a job with an electronics firm but the employer later discovers a deficiency in some specific applied skill, the graduate-under-warranty can simply return to the college for the few days or weeks required to be trained for that very specific skill. Continuing adult education is the course each of us is enrolled in — and examples like this one from PEI help us see the smart ways we can integrate learning with earning a living.

More than the ability to work with the latest tools and technologies, however, Canadian workers also need to be liberated by being entrusted with more responsibility. Front-line workers who can make decisions themselves, rather than always having to check with the boss, will become more involved and accountable for what they are doing.

In many successful Canadian businesses today, the new approaches of front-line decision-making, of working groups or teams, of employee choice with respect to upgrading skills and solving problems, have all awakened within many individuals a new sense of interest in what they are doing. These approaches also kindle a greater sense of responsibility for one's work and duties.

It is probably safe to say that most people are not only looking for the necessary paycheque at the end of the week, but also for a personal sense of fulfilment in what they are doing.

There is an entrepreneurial instinct in most people which, if given an opportunity to be realized, can unleash tremendous energy into their lives and the businesses where they work. Yet this certainly requires an attitude on the part of employers and management to see workers as individuals with tremendous potential.

An easy way to know whether a company has this liberating attitude is to visit its offices or plant operations and witness the attitude and atmosphere. Another way is to look at the annual reports of companies, and see whether along with the pictures of the officers there are any photographs of employees in the plant or office or laboratory, or whether they are unidentified, seen as just another no-name part of the infrastructure. In an entrepreneurial democracy, many incentives exist to bring the best out of people — from the simple act of recognition of workers as individuals, through procedures for initiative and decision-making at the front line or in work teams, and on to profit sharing.

This business culture has been the cause of such Canadian success stories as Magna International, whose chairman Frank Stronach "opens the books" to employees; under the company's constitution those who earned the profits get a share of them. There's something for everyone — workers, managers, shareholders, charity, research, reinvestment, and the taxman. Moreover, the workers know they have a say in the operations — and those operations, through good times and bad, have been supported and are successful.

THE PROPER PLACE OF PRIVATE ENTERPRISE

Taken together these three elements — open markets, debt reduction, and the empowerment of Canadian workers — are vital in moving forward to renewal. In the process it will be important to enlist business as an ally, rather than to distrust the private sector as an enemy, an attitude frequently found in Canada and reflected in some public policy.

At the same time, it will be necessary in cutting government spending to eliminate many of the grants, subsidies, and special concessions made by government to business. We have already witnessed too much private enterprise at public expense.

Most of the information on this chapter about Canada's debt crisis is truly depressing. Unfortunately, much more could be said about how severe and deep-seated our problem is. For example, there is the still unabated expectation by many Canadians that we can continue to operate the world's most generous welfare system on the back of a debilitated economy, as dramatically demonstrated recently by the falling-out between unions and the NDP government in Ontario. Space does not permit the whole bleak story to be included here.

Yet as desperate as any situation appears, there is always reason for hope. For me, one of the hopeful signs of what is possible for us in our present dilemma comes from the recent history of Mexico.

Many Canadians probably remember the shock waves sent throughout world financial markets in 1982 when Mexico announced that it was simply not going to make any further payments on its foreign debts. Mexico had reached the crisis point, crushed beneath its burden of debt.

Today, Mexico is in an extremely healthy financial position and is running a budget surplus. What happened? How did this country move so dramatically from night to day, from crisis to renewal?

The arrival of President Salinas meant more than just a new face in office. It signalled a wholesale change in approach to public finance, government operations, and financial accountability. Decisive action by Salinas and his like-minded supporters to cut the heavy weight of government borrowing for programs and services that the country could not afford, and to eliminate many organizations and structures that were impeding economic growth, set Mexico on a new pathway.

The old protectionist policies that had safeguarded a stagnating Mexican economy for all the decades of this century were dismantled, and Salinas actively sought open markets with the United States and Canada as a fundamental part of his program for economic renewal. We have the inspiration of his and Mexico's success right here on our own continent.

Where there is a will — and a coherent economic plan — there is a way.

CHAPTER THREE

Canadian Patriotism (There Is Such a Thing)

W HAT DOES IT REALLY MEAN to be a Canadian? This simple question needs to be thoughtfully considered, and answered, as we seek the renewal of our country.

We've been a long time developing our identity as Canadians. As a people made up of fragments from many different cultures and countries, we know that one of our defining attributes is our diversity. Often our identity has been expressed in terms of our relationship with places beyond our borders, such as Great Britain during the days of Empire, or more recently the United States. Our preoccupation with Canadian identity even gave rise to a royal commission on the subject in the 1950s, as Canadian an enterprise as one could ever imagine!

Keeping our country united has long been an imperative of those in government at Ottawa, and the past several decades have seen tremendous efforts to seek greater Canadian unity by means of changing our Constitution. Endless efforts, and countless conferences, have produced a country whose people have grown fatigued by proposals to rewrite an existing Constitution. Certainly this was an avenue pursued with great energy and effort by the Mulroney government, which led to both the Meech Lake Accord and the subsequent Charlottetown Accord, neither of which ultimately resulted in any changes to the Constitution.

WHAT CANADA NEEDS — A CULTURAL RE-CONFEDERATION

In fact the approach to a more unified country lies, I believe, along a different route all together. In his last public speech, at the University of Toronto, the late Northrop Frye said it succinctly: "What Canada needs is not more constitutional tinkering, but a cultural re-confederation."

Much greater emphasis on the cultural dimensions of Canadian life will awaken a justifiable pride in our country. There are many Canadian stories, and they deserve to be told. The Canadian Broadcasting Corporation has long been an instrument for binding Canadians together through the sharing of these Canadian stories, holding a mirror to the many different parts of our nation. Yet in recent years the ever-present onslaught of non-Canadian stories, in movies and television and magazines and music, particularly from the United States, have displaced the story of our Canada within.

Over recent years we have been concentrating on becoming more competitive economically in the international marketplace, on entering into trade treaties, and on expanding our commercial activities. In the process we have neglected the cultural dimension of Canadian life. Better trading arrangements, greater economic competitiveness, and improvements in the taxation system are vitally important, but they are not goals in themselves. They are means to an end, ways of achieving the objective of being a strong and free and sovereign Canadian people.

When I was expressing my belief about the need for a more vibrant Canadian patriotism on Andy Barrie's CFRB radio phone-in show on March 19, 1993, a caller explained her agreement. She had worked with the Spicer Commission and had "listened to many thousands of Canadians, none of whom had any idea of who they really are."

From my own observations over the past several years, I have concluded that many Canadians seem to think they are Americans who simply happen to be located north of the border. I listen to speeches in the House of Commons where Canadian parliamentarians use American examples to describe Canadian situations. I listen to Canadians who watch American television, following the U.S. presidential election and stating their preferences between Bush, Clinton, and Perot, as if they were American voters rather than Canadians who ought to filter American politics through the crucial question, "What impact will this man and his policies have on Canada?" Quite apart from cross-border shopping, many Canadians routinely vacation in the United States but have not yet visited most parts of our own country.

Probably the most depressing call I received from a constituent came late one evening. His irate complaint was that he could no longer get American football on the Buffalo television station that had just been bumped from the Toronto channels to make way for a second French-language channel. What really bothered me was that the constituent in question was the principal of a local school, someone in charge of the education of a whole new generation of Canadian children.

TELLING OUR OWN STORIES TO OURSELVES

The government of Canada can do much to encourage the telling of our Canadian story to Canadians. It doesn't even take a lot of money to do so, although a fraction of the amount spent over the past two decades on constitutional conferencing will now produce a far more unified country when spent on the cultural dimensions of our life.

The area of Canadian broadcasting is a good example of how bad we have become. A recent study by UNESCO ranks Canada last out of 79 countries in the amount of broadcast time devoted to its own cultural programming. The total amount of Canadian programming watched by Canadians is a meagre 4.4%. The Canadian broadcasting industry, notably lacking any patriotic sentiment, busily engages in bringing popular American TV programs into Canadian homes. In those cases where Canada's private broadcasters produce "Canadian content" material, they do so, according to Peter Herrndorf, chairman of TVOntario, with the motivation of resale into the U.S. market, instead of making a concentrated effort to mirror Canadian society.

In cultural programming, Mr. Herrndorf told a CRTC hearing on the future of Canadian television in March 1993, Canadian producers, directors, and writers are "finding it more and more difficult to find the airtime and the resources to provide viewers with a Canadian perspective in these areas."

Another voice at the same CRTC hearing, that of Arnold Amber, president of the Association of Television Producers and Directors, proposed that the government should give up trying to impose Canadian content requirements and instead follow the example of the Europeans and build a true public broadcasting service, financed from public funds held by Telefilm Canada and provincial agencies and a tax levied through the cable system.

As Canadian observer Michael Valpy has lamented, "We don't need to be 79th out of 79, do we?" Every study, every royal commission, every parliamentary debate on broadcasting since the 1920s has concluded that Canada's cultural and political sovereignty is tied to the existence of a broadcasting system that is predominantly Canadian. Yet the unmistakable and lamentable trend of the past decade has been the increase in the Americanization of Canadian broadcasting. When it comes to protecting Canadian sovereignty, a wise government with $5.8-billion to spend might choose Canadian broadcasting over anti-submarine helicopters.

LET CANADIANS SHARE MORE DIRECTLY THE BENEFITS OF CULTURAL SUBSIDIES

Another way to increase the Canadian content in the lives of our citizens would be to change the way funding is given to the arts and cultural communities in Canada. Currently, subsidies are given directly to authors and publishers, or to theatre companies, or dance troupes, or museums and galleries. A variation of a marketplace approach could provide the same amount of money to these groups and organizations but in way that would involve the Canadian people far more. For example, instead of a grant to a book publisher, the same amount of money could be committed to buy several thousand copies of the book. This minimum guarantee purchase would help the publisher keep the unit price down as he expands the size of the press run for the book to include the number he would normally expect to sell through the bookstores and to libraries. The author would get his or her money in royalties on books sold. The copies purchased by the government could be distributed in various ways to Canadian taxpayers, who would end up having some tangible benefits from the exercise.

Similarly for theatrical companies, government funding could be used to purchase tickets for several weeks of a full house, and the tickets could be, once again, distributed or raffled off to taxpayers in the community. It might even be the first time that a "winner" had attended a stage play, and perhaps mark the start of a new interest in attending theatre. The same concept could apply for admission tickets to art galleries and museums.

The idea here can be refined in its various applications, I have no doubt, but the concept simply is to ensure that where public money is spent on Canadian artistic and cultural activities, inventive new approaches be used to ensure that taxpaying Canadians actually have the possibility of benefiting from the exercise. It's in everybody's interest — especially when our purpose is a cultural re-confederation, a new awakening to who we really are.

VISITING A FOREIGN LAND — CANADA!

Airfares and other transportation costs are designed, it seems, to encourage Canadians to fly to Europe or the United States, rather than journey to destinations within our own country — another way we inhibit greater awareness of who we Canadians really are.

I have always been inspired by the way Canadians who discover other parts of our country become excited about the beauty and diversity, and about the fine qualities of the people they have met. Invariably, their experiences are a blending of surprise and pleasure — especially upon realizing that the area they visited is also a part of their very own country.

In 1992 a low-budget exchange of Canadian youth was organized, with up to 125 youngsters aged sixteen to twenty-one from each of Canada's 295 constituencies visiting their "twins" for one week. I arranged for the voyageurs from my Etobicoke-

Lakeshore constituency to visit northwest Saskatchewan, since I had worked there as a newspaper reporter myself in my early twenties and wanted them to experience the same discoveries I had made twenty-five years earlier. At first I was concerned to discover the clear lack of enthusiasm which youngsters in my riding displayed about going there. The prospect held modest appeal for them, at best. Yet once the exchange was over they had become fast friends with their twins in North Battleford, Loon Lake, and tiny Debden. They have since become avid pen pals, sending one another videotapes, and organizing exchange reunions all at their own expense.

Of course it does not take organized programs to move Canadians around inside our vast country; individuals are free to do this themselves. Yet encouragement, good examples, and even non-financial incentives can help.

A Canadian Youth Service Corps

What about creating an organization for Canadian youth that would become a major vehicle for awakening in younger Canadians a sense of patriotism through service? When the Hon. Benoit Bouchard on behalf of the Mulroney government cancelled the Katimavik Program several years ago, he pledged that the government "would replace it with something even better." The time to do so has arrived.

For several years I have been working on plans for the creation of a Canadian Youth Service Corps and have advocated the concept in Parliament and elsewhere. The corps would provide one year of opportunity for young Canadians, generally following high school and before university. Planning can continue, and implementation begin, when the spending moratorium ends.

The Canadian Youth Service Corps could comprise several divisions or "streams" suitable for the different interests and aptitudes of the youth who enlist. One stream would be for environmental service, and activities could range from reforestation projects to clean-up and conservation efforts and projects relating to endangered species.

A second stream would be for military-type service, a kind of first-stage boot camp for younger Canadians wanting to acquire discipline and physical conditioning, as well as some basic training. This stream would be valuable for those hoping eventually to become members of the Reserves or Regular Forces. This stream of training would also be ideal for those wishing to pursue careers in policing, fire-fighting, or other emergency services.

A third stream would be for social service, particularly appropriate for young Canadians intending to continue their education for a career in any of the helping professions. In this stream, for instance, many of the human and social needs in our communities could be responded to by the youth, such as working with seniors, assisting people with disabilities, providing company to shut-ins.

A fourth stream would be public service, in which youth could work in various government departments, particularly those involving the need for large manpower resources in field projects.

A fifth stream could relate to service abroad, patterned on the experience of Canadian University Students Overseas (CUSO) or possibly incorporating CUSO operations within the larger Canadian Youth Service Corps program.

The corps would operate on a rotational basis, so that during the year of enlistment a member would have three four-month tours of duty in different parts of Canada. Academic credit for the year of service could be granted, in arrangements worked out with Canada's educational authorities. This could echo the Antigonish Movement, which held that learning in the real world could be just as valuable as learning in the classroom.

Canada has prior experience with similar organizations, such as the Company of Young Canadians, Katimavik, and the Environmental Youth Corps of Alberta. The experience of the YMCA and YWCA organizations in Canada would also prove helpful in the formation of the youth corps. The Scouting and Guiding movements, as well as church youth organizations, provide some lessons and models for training in self-reliance and service to others. The military stream of the corps could lean heavily on the expertise of the Canadian Armed Forces, which have good working models with the Air Cadets, Sea Cadets, and Summer Soldiers programs.

Canada is required to close a number of military bases due to reduction in the size of the Canadian Armed Forces; some of these existing facilities could alternately be used by the Youth Service Corps.

As challenging as the corps will be for Canadian youth, it can also give a new lease on life for adult Canadians who take up the leadership roles in the organization. A great many Canadians who know this country well and have valuable experience and skills, love to work with young people. I'm thinking especially of those who have reached a stage in life where personal financial security is no longer a preoccupation, and who are interested in doing something new and valuable with their lives (especially as they experience the shock of mid-life when those special anniversary birthdays are encountered!).

People sometimes wonder what the differences really are between Canadians and Americans. I first began working on this youth corps proposal while at the Aspen Institute in

Colorado (within its extensive John F. Kennedy Library where I read the original drafts and documents of the concept that eventually became Kennedy's Peace Corps). I asked all the Americans I encountered whether they thought such a corps should be compulsory. Invariably, they said yes. Back in Canada, however, the unanimous response was that such a program should be voluntary only. We Canadians can rise to the occasion, and we love to provide service to others (witness the extremely high level of voluntarism supporting thousands of non-profit and community organizations across our country), but we do not like to be told what to do!

Canada as Others See Us

We get a better perspective on ourselves by noting what foreigners observe about our country. Their general view of Canada is of a successful, peaceful, and civilized nation. Even shy Canadians, typically shuffling the ground with our feet or tugging on our forelock, showed a bit of pride when the news came in last year that the United Nations ranked our country first among all countries in the world. This ranking was based on criteria about the quality of life and comprehensive nature of social and educational programs and opportunities.

Frankly, I always thought that our diffident sense about ourselves serves as a good antidote to pomposity. We seldom let anybody get too high up the ladder before we point out his or her faults. We are not a nation of hero worshippers. Humility is a respectable Canadian virtue.

It is one thing to be modest, though, and quite another to lack self-confidence. I believe that our consistent inability to reinforce our common Canadianism has prevented us from enjoying the benefits of a positive spirit of patriotism.

Consider, for example, how others see us when it comes to Canadian representation abroad. Most countries establish embassies and consulates overseas to represent the national interest in those lands with whom they have diplomatic relations. Not so in the case of Canada. We muddy the water by having *provincial* missions in other countries, along with the government of Canada's representation. What is the image of "Canada" in Britain, France, or the United States, for instance, when in these countries offices are to be found flying provincial flags and carrying such names as Ontario House, Quebec House, Alberta House, Nova Scotia House? Now that the budget crunch is upon us and provincial governments are driven to stop spending money they don't have, they would do well to be rid of this pretension, and fold their foreign operations into the overseas missions of the government of Canada. It's time we presented a Canadian face to the world.

REDEFINING OUR RELATIONSHIP WITH THE UNITED STATES

One of the enduring issues facing Canada is the nature of our relationship with the United States.

Over the long course of our history, the moods surrounding this relationship ebb and flow, depending in part on the cycles of Canadian and American nationalism. We pass through eras of trade reciprocity, followed by periods of trade protection, followed by further periods of opening up markets and forging stronger commercial ties. Canadian-American relations also are influenced by overseas wars (such as Canada's resentment in the early part of World War II when America stayed out, followed by a common bond against the adversary when America joined the Alliance against the fascist Axis powers).

During the Cold War, Canadians generally felt very comfortable in NATO and NORAD with the umbrella of protective defence shared with the all-powerful American military.

Now that the Cold War has ended and more independence is again possible in the foreign policy of many countries, including Canada, we find some pressures for divergence from the U.S. Yet these are coinciding with continental pressures for economic and cultural convergence with the Americans. So we have come to a time again in Canadian history where it is important to redefine our relationship with our southern neighbour.

The development of a heightened awareness of who and what we are as Canadians is essential to this process. We can only define, and then defend, Canadian national interests when we have some basic consensus among ourselves as to just what those interests are.

The advantages we have already gained under the Canada-U.S. Free Trade Agreement, by having a panel that hears and resolves trade disputes between our two countries, has been tremendously important in bringing fairness into our trading relationship. Never in history has there been so much trade and commerce operated between two countries as is the case today between Canada and the United States. In fact there is even more trade between the province of Ontario and the state of New York than there is between the United States and Japan. Given the millions of transactions, and the extensive economic and commercial interactions, it is inevitable that some disputes arise. Although Americans perhaps think of themselves as free market traders, they have in fact expressed a strong protectionist sentiment. Many non-tariff barriers exist, and a thoughtful and determined effort by Canadians and the government of Canada is required to overcome this.

Goodwill is the best basis for the relationship between our two countries, and so is the respect that will be earned when, in those cases where it is necessary, the government of Canada speaks clearly and forthrightly in defence of Canadian interests — on diverse matters from American activities in our Arctic waters to trade retaliation on Canadian steel exports to the USA.

Canadians continue to be fascinated by the excitement and dynamic diversity of the United States, while being repelled by the excesses for which that country is also widely known, such as violence and widespread use of firearms. The story of Canada's evolution has always been one of an involved and complicated relationship with the United States, beginning when Britain's thirteen most populous and prosperous colonies rebelled against the Crown and in their victory created an independent republic, leaving the more northerly colonies behind as "British" North America — the basis of present-day Canada. No doubt Canada would have evolved as a very different country, especially in our cultural sense of being and our national integrity, if we had been more isolated and developed on our own; if, for instance, the United States was simply not present as our neighbour and constant counterpoint. The evolution of Australia, a country like Canada in so many ways (having a federal state, a parliamentary democracy, a constitutional monarchy, European settlement encountering an aboriginal population, a vast land mass sparsely populated), makes quite a comparison. It is also quite a contrast. Australians developed a stronger sense of identity because, unlike Canada, they had no powerful neighbouring nation in relation to which everything was constantly being measured.

Who we are as Canadians is closely intertwined with the Americans, but it need not take the form of hostile anti-Americanism or a chauvinistic Canadian nationalism. We do not want nor do we need to be anti-American, but more positively, we should and must be strongly pro-Canadian.

You Are Who Your Name Says You Are

It has been observed that individuals take on certain attributes over time in response to their names. Even the attitude of others toward a person can be influenced somewhat by his or her name. For instance, a fellow thinks differently about himself depending on whether he is called "Billy" or "William." In an odd way, the same applies to our country, and is one of the reasons so many Canadians seem to have an unclear identity or image of who we are.

I am referring to the fact that mostly you hear reference to "the federal government," and even more annoyingly "the feds," when in truth people are referring to the Government of Canada. For a long time we used the word "Dominion" in this connection, and everyone knew that the Dominion or Dominion Government meant our whole country. Yet such a lacklustre substitute as "federal" is just one more of the many contributing factors to our out-of-focus image of Canada.

While this point might strike some as trivial, I believe that by referring to our national government only as the Government of Canada from now on, we will gradually see a rising sense of awareness and identity, since this designation refers to an entity far more concrete and comprehensible.

Beyond Multiculturalism to Canadianism

A recent telephone exchange in my constituency office:

"What is Mr. Boyer's nationality?" inquired the voice on the telephone.

"He is a Canadian," replied my assistant.

"No, I mean what is his national origin?" pressed the caller, explaining that she was working on a research project on the ethnic background of Toronto-area MPs.

"Well, you'd better just put down that he is Canadian," repeated my assistant, who knows my views about this sort of thing.

We will never amount to much in this country until we think of ourselves as Canadians.

Multiculturalism has been a most important stage in our development. Recognition of the truly diverse origins of the people who are now citizens of Canada has certainly broadened the awareness of what it means to be a "Canadian," and our emphasis on multiculturalism over the past decade or so has succeeded in breaking down stereotypes of who "qualifies" as a real Canadian.

Yet I believe the time has come to move forward to the next stage in our evolution as a human society, to what I would call an integrating Canadianism.

To become more aware of ourselves as Canadians, we can now let go of some concepts that were intended to help but which in fact have divided us. Emotionally and psychologically, we also ought to help one another just to relax and genuinely enjoy what and who we are as Canadians. In the absence of phoney standards, and free of being uptight about our differences, we can discover a special sense of kinship.

"Let us celebrate our diversity" was a slogan Johnny Lombardi developed at CHIN ratio station in Toronto to promote his multi-language broadcasts. It was a perfect theme for his popular station. Yet Jim Flemming, a Toronto-area Liberal MP and Minister of State for Multiculturalism, then adopted these five words for Ottawa's approach in the early 1980s.

While the phrase "celebrating diversity" was a helpful way to portray a tolerant spirit, a good radio slogan does not necessarily make good national policy. I say instead: "Let us celebrate our Canadianism."

We who are citizens of Canada share more in common than we have differences that divide us. If we would talk more about our shared strengths and common interests, there will be less separatism. When we stop emphasizing our diversity, we will stop feeding racism and resentment.

Canada as a "mosaic" is another term frequently used to describe us. This concept came from the work of sociologist John Porter, whose years of research on the structure of Canadian society was published in his landmark book *The Vertical Mosaic* in 1965. While this phrase, too, was helpful to portray something of the sociological make-up of Canada, a good sociologist's term does not necessarily make good national policy, either. We cannot substitute either slogans or descriptions for the passion and the idealism we should feel in being Canadians.

Too much emphasis on diversity and differences creates the basis, or the excuse, for keeping some people in a category of second-class citizens. Instead, when we promote the reality that we are all Canadians, we form the intellectual and social context for acceptance of everyone as equals.

An attitude of acceptance brings energy and life to the formal legal equality that now exists among all Canadians, and it helps to ensure that we will never obscure the rights and importance of minorities within our country. (Our Charter of Rights and Freedoms now guarantees, in article 15, our legal equality. Each one of us is equal before and under the law, has the right to equal benefit of the law, and to equal protection of the law — without discrimination, including discrimination on the basis of race, national or ethnic origin, colour, religion, sex, age, or mental or physical disability. This is the *legal* basis of integrated Canadianism. Yet the *spirit* of the law, as well as its letter, ultimately must triumph.

We must remain vigilant, in the words of a poem I remember from public school days, to "curb the strong and uphold the weak." This was the spirit of the recommendations in the Parliamentary Committee on Equality Rights which I chaired, and whose report to Parliament I submitted in 1985, entitled "Equality for All."

It is the essence of the work we must do in Parliament and elsewhere for and with the 3,300,000 Canadians with varying degrees of mental and physical disabilities. It is the conscience that now directs all Canadians to seek justice for Canada's First Peoples. It is the hope that will inspire all of us — including the original "Canadians" — to welcome living in a common home where linguistic and cultural differences are not feared but enjoyed.

This is the future we have as Canadians, whatever our origins, however or whenever we each came to be here. Each of us is a member of some minority group or other, and while that must continue to be respected, we have reached the point in our evolution as a society where the pendulum ought now to swing again toward fuller recognition that everyone of us is, above all, a Canadian.

Thirty years have passed since John Diefenbaker — who appointed the first woman to a Canadian cabinet and the first native Indian to the Senate, whose government was supported by the first black Canadian and the first Canadian of Chinese origin ever elected to the House of Commons, who appointed a Jew to be governor of the Bank of Canada at a time when Canadian banking was a closed shop to Jews, who gave native Canadians the right to vote for the first time, who always fought for the underdog and gave us the

Canadian Bill of Rights — urged us to accept "unhyphenated" Canadianism. It's time to end hyphenitis.

Pride in our origins ought not to take precedence over the reality that we are all now Canadians.

It is interesting to know something about another person's background, including where they, or their ancestors, came from. Canadian historian W.L. Morton, writing about the personality attributes of conservatives, once suggested that a conservative instinctively wants to know the background of a person, where she grew up, or where his family came from. Because we are all part of our past, this constructive curiosity does help form a clearer picture of someone. Yet we must not make the mistake of trying to transform something that is valid for some individual at the personal level into a national policy.

I have criticized the Canada census form because it goes into great detail about a person's national origin, but leaves, almost as a bureaucratic afterthought, limited space for a citizen to be shown as "Canadian."

What value is it to the researcher who phoned my office to know about the national or ethnic background of MPs? Wouldn't it be more important to know what values MPs stand for, what programs they're advocating, and what success they've had in trying to accomplish their goals?

Canadian soldiers in the past developed a spirit of camaraderie, and a sense of shared purpose, regardless of where in our country they came from, regardless of their national background. They all wore, and saw on each other, the shoulder patch that simply read "CANADA."

The best way for us to live up to the challenge and the promise of this vast country of ours, and the most positive way to start thinking and working together, is for each of us to say: "I am a Canadian."

CHAPTER FOUR

What Canadians Want

BACK IN THE COLD WAR DAYS, considerations of security were most often expressed in terms of national defence and anti-espionage activity. Today the focus of security has become much more personal. The threat most people feel is not nuclear war but a lack of personal security: individual safety, financial security, and well-being in a world of environmental threats and economic dislocations. Now, more than ever, we should focus on the personal security of individuals.

In the past, too many of our policies and programs have been examined in terms of how they affect governments, and much of the heat and debate over public policy is really just a turf war between different levels of government within Canada. The real test, in my view, ought to be how government programs and services are experienced in the life of individual Canadians, measured in terms of their own needs and seen from their own perspectives within this country.

Four areas in which this focus on personal security can bring new meaning and relevance to individual Canadians are law and order, the environment, employment, and financial security.

LAW AND ORDER

On the law-and-order front, major changes have been adopted by the government of Canada and Parliament, ranging from the Young Offenders Act to extradition, parole, protection of victims, and firearms and dangerous offenders. These initiatives, which have resulted in tightening up the system for more effective criminal justice, must be fully carried forward — indeed must receive even stronger emphasis.

Dangerous offenders represent a particular threat to the safety of individuals and our communities. Recent experience has tragically shown that those convicted of certain patterns of crime must remain isolated from society, however much rehabilitation and psychological monitoring they may have received. The 1993 recommendations from the Parliamentary Justice Committee, chaired by Dr. Bob Horner, correctly point to the strict new discipline that must apply in this area.

The Mulroney government's amendments to the Young Offenders Act in May 1992 shifted the primary focus from the previous concern for the interests of the offender to a new higher concern for the protection of society. So, too, when it comes to dangerous offenders, protection of society must be paramount. This feeling is deeply held by Canadians, and their views should be reflected in the laws and procedures making up our criminal justice system. Following the tragic murder of youngsters in our country, often involving sexual abuse, many thousands of Canadians are signing petitions requesting reinstatement of capital punishment for those convicted of killing children.

I voted in Parliament for reinstatement of capital punishment. It is clear to me that there are cases of premeditated murder (such as by the individual who plants a bomb aboard an airplane and kills two or three hundred innocent people) where the appropriate sanction is capital punishment. What about cases where murder may not be premeditated or committed in "cold blood" because the killer is not mentally or psychologically responsible for their acts? There is no less need here to protect society and ensure that the criminal justice system holds accountable the one who has left behind a victim and a circle of tragedy. If capital punishment is not to be considered appropriate for such criminals, there must at a minimum be certainty that such dangerous offenders will never again be free to prey on others.

This situation does not require further study. The Justice Committee has already been clear on how to deal with dangerous sexual offenders. Rather than seeking to "buy time" on this issue, we now must purchase a fuller measure of personal security for Canadian individuals by implementing a stricter regime to prevent release of dangerous offenders back into society.

The 1992 amendments to the Young Offenders Act, marking the second time the Mulroney government had sought to tighten up this controversial legislation, now appear to be successfully removing some of the worst abuses, specifically the way that hardened young criminals could escape public identification or appropriate sanction for their crimes. The maximum sentence for murder, where the accused is a young offender, has been increased from three to five years. Cases involving young offenders can now be more readily transferred to adult court, where the special immunities for youngsters would not apply. The act now directs judges to place safety of the community in higher priority to the interests of the accused, an important reversal, as mentioned above, from the previous ranking in the act.

The hard-edged nature of anti-social and anti-human activity by some youngsters in Canadian society continues to distress many Canadians. We are reaping the sour harvest of family violence, of lack of purpose, and of cultural disintegration. You cannot present to formative young minds an endless procession of violence and human degradation, whether on television or in movies or in society, and not produce violent attitudes and unfeeling actions. The tragedy here was pathetically summed up recently in the unapologetic words of a young murderer, "We were only doing it for fun." On the same day in March 1993 that people were shocked to learn how two ten-year-old boys had kidnapped and murdered a trusting two-year-old child in England, a senior citizen in my electoral district was assaulted by an eight-year-old boy.

It is not only in the enactment of more stringent criminal laws, but also in a profound contest within the deepest elements of our culture, that we must renew ourselves in focusing on respect for life and the personal security of individuals.

The violence done against the image of women and children in pornography, and the denigration of human dignity in the explicit illustration of violence in so much of the art and entertainment of our times, remind us again of the important need for censorship. I am amazed, in the never-ending struggle to maintain a balance between the personal security of individuals and the freedom of artistic expression, to hear people urge that there be no censorship whatsoever. From Plato to the present, valid reasons have been advanced about the need to protect society from the vicious and sick elements within it. Seeing what ends up on the clipping room floor at the censor's office — including scenes of chainsaw murders and death-inflicting procedures in snuff movies — would persuade any Canadian of common sense that we can do better than to enshrine in our cultural life the lowest elements of degenerate behaviour.

The bleak tragedies of our human society are harsh enough, and the damning verdict on our twentieth century will take account of the organized torture and death brutally inflicted, sometimes in random madness but too often in systematically organized fashion, on millions of innocent souls. There is much to be reckoned for. Which is why both in atonement and in defiant celebration of life, we do better not to mimic death and encourage violence against people and nature, but rather to uplift, celebrate, inspire. Where is our nobility?

ENVIRONMENTAL PROTECTION

The environmental degradation of our planet has also passed from being one of general to personal concern. For instance, when mothers cannot let their children play in the sunny backyard because of harmful ultraviolet radiation, due to depletion of the protective ozone layer, personal security can truly mean "in my backyard."

Many initiatives under the government of Canada's Green Plan are properly focused on this threat. Measures removing lead from gasoline and chlorofluorocarbons from aerosol sprays, Canada's landmark legislation that treats the entire lifecycle of hazardous and toxic substances, major initiatives in clean-up and new emphasis on recycling — all are part of the steps that must be taken to reassert security of all living beings on this planet. In most cases, moreover, these threats are ones that can be addressed by each of us, with our individual actions cumulatively producing a transformation.

These are valuable programs and initiatives from the Mulroney years which must now be carried vigorously forward. Much remains to be done in overcoming our past patterns of environmental degradation, all the more so as we focus on the personal security of individuals: the quality of the air we breathe, the safety of the water we drink.

We know that the lifestyle which most Canadians developed over the past few decades is not sustainable.

The environmental ethic that has been emerging in recent years sees humans as part of the ecosystem and dependent on it rather than masters of it. This awareness has emerged for good reason. Consider the farmlands of central Canada where overuse of pesticides and chemical fertilizers has spelt contamination; clear-cut forestry in British Columbia that has ravaged the landscape and wastefully depleted resources; and the overexploitation of the North Atlantic fishery causing the extinction of species of marine life and, as a result, the recent closing of the cod fishery.

For the past three years, I have been closely associated with an important environmental initiative, the formation of the International Green Cross, a new organization that would respond to environmental disasters in much the same way the International Red Cross responds to human needs in times of emergency. This will be a *non*-governmental organization.

Since 1990 I have been meeting with people from many countries who share this new vision of a global organization that can provide timely and effective response to environmental emergencies. Frequently writing and speaking about the need for an International Green Cross, I have received a large measure of interest and support from many quarters. Canadians see such an entity as being what our country at its best is all about: a practical and technically effective operation to do something tangible in response to a real need.

At the Earth Summit in Rio de Janiero in June 1992, I participated with many environmental leaders from other countries in advancing plans for this organization. Mikhail

Gorbachev, former president of the Soviet Union, is chairing our international committee for the Green Cross, and parliamentarians in many countries are now working to bring this organization into being.

EMPLOYMENT

Many men and women who once felt secure in their employment, because they held jobs in institutions or large corporations, are finding that in reality they, too, are vulnerable. The competitive new international marketplace, combined with ever-faster changes in technology and automation, means many jobs are simply evaporating.

As we emerge from this recession, it won't be "business as usual." The world has changed. The Mulroney government brought legislation before Parliament transforming the Unemployment Insurance system to incorporate an active program of retraining. As a result, some $2.21-billion of UI funds will be used in 1993 to help some 530,000 unemployed Canadians upgrade their skills and return to work. We also introduced the Canada Scholarship Program so that many thousands of students can now train in advanced science and technology. We created the Centres of Excellence in Industry and Technology to foster Canadian growth in areas of national strength. We have aggressively pursued new trading opportunities through the Free Trade Agreement and the North American Free Trade Agreement to ensure that the export of manufactured goods and services means more and better jobs here at home.

Government policies in this area of technical education, skills enhancement, and better jobs will succeed best when they are focused, in their application, on the level of the personal dynamic of individual workers. Individual Canadian workers, with their need for financial security and for personal recognition and responsibility, are the real sparks in the coming economic renewal.

FINANCIAL SECURITY

Canadians on fixed incomes and those in advancing years fear they may lose their jobs. They feel greater vulnerability in these uncertain times.

The best news for those on fixed incomes is that the government's goal of zero inflation is getting results. Inflation is now at a thirty-year low. In terms of support and security, the government of Canada is now spending $36-billion more on social expenditures than in 1984 — an amount that in fact must be reviewed to ensure that these programs are sustainable in financial terms.

Despite this record, some people still fall through the social safety net. Many people who relied on temporary transitional assistance, such as unemployment insurance, are becoming more and more dependent on social assistance. That is why the Mulroney government has worked to reorient existing programs to promote full participation — for example, by creating the new Child Tax Benefit, effective January 1, 1993. This intelligently combines the old family allowances, child credit, and refundable child tax credit into a single, non-taxable benefit for low-income and middle-income families, focusing public spending on those who truly need it.

Similarly, Canadians who find themselves in the welfare trap, unable to get work and out of UI benefits, deserve a better system. There is very little incentive for people to try to get off welfare (other than their personal feeling of being in a situation they wish to escape) when their minor earnings from some temporary work are deducted from their welfare payments: at the end of the month they are probably in the same position financially, so where's the incentive to work? Without putting a single cent more into existing welfare support payments, the government of Canada could dramatically revamp the system to provide far more financial security for individuals, and give them incentive to earn money and improve their lot at the same time.

A recent proposal by Conservative MP Al Johnson of Calgary points clearly in this direction. Johnson calls his plan the "simple, progressive tax" (SPT). The SPT would provide income support of $4,000 to each person (man, woman or child). In addition, each family with at least one child under eighteen would receive "family" income support of an additional $4,500. These income support payments would not be taxed. A second element of the SPT plan is a flat rate tax. All income earned by anyone is taxed equally, essentially without deduction, at a combined Canadian-provincial rate of 40%.

The income support payments that form the basis of the SPT system would replace government of Canada contributions to social assistance and payments under the unemployment insurance system. Provinces would be free to use their existing social assistance budgets to supplement the Canadian SPT program, or they could chose to allocate their funding toward helping and healing programs such as low-income housing, child care, safe homes for victims of abuse, and similar forms of non-taxable assistance.

I believe this SPT integrated income support and tax concept could lead the way to genuine renewal, and give new hope to many Canadians who are struggling to provide for their basic financial security.

In my work as Member of Parliament for Etobicoke-Lakeshore, I have focused over the past eight years on policies and programs that relate to the security of the individual. Initiatives on behalf of Canadians with mental and physical disabilities have accordingly been an important part of my public work. So have programs flowing from my committee's 1985 report "Equality for All," aimed at upholding weaker or more vulnerable members of our society. Providing income supplements (based on need) for widows between ages sixty and sixty-five, who had none and who had been essentially forgotten, was a real accomplishment which I strongly supported. Now is the time, more than ever, to emphasize this focus.

The personal feeling of security experienced by each individual in our country is a good measure of how civilized we are. Whether the vulnerable person is a child, a person with disabilities, an elderly or infirm Canadian, an unemployed and aging worker, or a woman exploited in the workplace or feeling at risk in the community — achieving that person's security will be the new measure of our success as a society.

CHAPTER FIVE

Listening to the People

THERE IS A FEELING among many Canadians today that governments and politicians are out for themselves and have lost contact with the people. Any living, breathing Canadian is aware of the mood of concern and distrust that has diminished the standing of elected representatives, or, if you say it sneeringly, "politicians."

The real cause of frustration with Canada's political system goes much deeper than the antics of political posturing during parliamentary Question Period, or even the inappropriate acts of some politicians that have led to scandals and criminal convictions. No, here is the source of the anger: *the fact that we have so much government doing so many things at such great cost — but still coming up short in terms of results.*

Happily it is true, as the United Nations recently reported, that Canada is the number-one country in the world in which to live. It is a fact that we have a high standard of living, high levels of education, and stability and order within our society — especially when compared with other countries.

Yet we are also aware of long-smouldering problems that have not been faced and until recently were hardly even acknowledged. The plight of Canada's First Peoples, the depletion of natural resources from the North Atlantic fishery to the clear-cut forests on our west coast, from the abuse of vulnerable people to the tax burden carried by law-abiding citizens who observe others freeloading off the system, from the anxiety of workers losing their jobs to changes in technology to the increase of mindless and violent crime — on and on goes the litany of our country's serious issues.

Every society has problems, to be sure. Many of the issues that Canadians grapple with today would no doubt seem, in most countries, inconsequential or even luxurious dilemmas. Yet in our country, and on our own terms, we do feel and believe that we can do better. This knowledge that we have not yet achieved our potential is the underlying reason for much discontent with our political system. Since this political system in turn is personified by individual elected representatives, we politicians become the easy lightning rod to receive the bolts of public anger.

THE GAP CAN BE CLOSED

I believe the gap between politicians and people can be closed. This is what Canadians are wanting more than anything else. Anyone who is genuinely listening to the people knows this.

There has been too much top-down government in Canada, which grew to its present swollen proportions because of the deferential attitude Canadians have traditionally had toward authority. Now this deference has disappeared. A new sense of the sovereignty of the people has emerged, creating the basis for a far more vigorous democracy.

Canadians definitely want more of a bottom-up or participatory approach in government. Yet it would be just as wrong to completely reverse the flow, to invert the present power relationship entirely. Twenty-seven million Canadians cannot directly and daily run the government of our country. What is called for, rather, *is a new partnership between those in government and the people*. This long-sought goal of a genuinely democratic society is now possible in Canada.

We're certainly not short of solutions to our problems. Perhaps no country in the world holds as many conferences and seminars to examine from so many angles the ways of resolving the items on our public agenda. Books, pamphlets, and committee reports abound, filled to overflowing with proposals and constructive suggestions. What we are short on is a process that involves people in choosing among those solutions and then helps them implement them and ensure their success.

The truth has finally dawned on us that without involvement, we don't get commitment. This is true in families, churches, offices, schools, unions, companies, and volunteer organizations, just as it is in government. Of course some people do like firm lines of direction, but when most people are told exactly what to do, they respond with indifference, or even hostility. Involvement becomes essential for success.

As people deliberate, and discuss, and even debate, then consensus becomes possible. We sometimes marvel at how the Chinese or Japanese are able to collectively come to a decision, after much deliberation, and then work relentlessly to carry their agreed-upon plan into action. This same consensus-building approach is also well known in the traditional decision-making patterns of many of Canada's First Peoples. Geoffrey York describes in his book *The Dispossessed: Life and Death in Native Canada* how the actions of the Manitoba chiefs, at the time of the decision to fight the Meech Lake Accord, "were formulated in a traditional system of consensus-building and collective decision-making. It was a unique form of democracy, with roots that stretched back for thousands of years." York noted how nobody could impose any decision on the chiefs. The issue before them was discussed collectively, and debate moved around the table until each chief had said as much as he wanted to say. The discussion continued until a consensus emerged. "The chiefs continually consulted their elders and the ordinary people in their communities," observed York, "to ensure that their decisions were broadly supported. It was a method that could serve as a model for democracy in Canada."

This slower approach may seem distasteful to Canadians in the fast lane, accustomed as they are to fast food and instant banking. Yet our recent political history has shown how some of the most costly mistakes made by government have been the result of decisions reached by a very small group, with little deliberation and certainly less public dialogue.

For a long time Canadian politics operated on the basis of a powerful attraction, on the part of those in government, to the "surprise announcement." Politicians of the day believed that a big news impact would enhance their public standing. In truth they were also afraid to face up to the realities of power sharing and the necessity of engaging in advance the people who would be affected by the decision, in case they objected or, even worse, rejected the proposal outright. Examples of "bold government" and "decisive leadership" have in fact too often been the story of government by just a handful of individuals, or even one powerful leader, and around this pattern or tradition has developed much supportive analysis and self-justifying mythology about the nature of political leadership.

Today in Canada we are ready to embrace a new concept of political leadership, based upon *empowerment of the people*. This will take many forms. It will change the way our country works, and the way we think about ourselves as Canadians. While the occasional direct voting by Canadian citizens in referendums will play a role in this, as will the power of citizens to initiate direct votes themselves on important public questions, these elements are only a small part of the transformation that is required.

A hands-on democracy must involve the trust of the people in a variety of ways. The goal in all cases, however, will be the same: to reconcile freedom with authority. This age-old problem will be much better addressed as we blend popular sovereignty with representative government.

This new approach would require putting major constitutional amendments directly to the people in a referendum for ratification. It would welcome measures to ensure greater worker control and greater worker participation in businesses where they are employed. It upholds the movement of shareholder democracy. It supports the concept of front-line decision-making. It seeks the active participation by the consumer of health care services, of information programs, or of job training, in how those programs and services apply in their specific case to their unique needs.

Here are just thirteen ways our political parties and governments can be more responsive to the people:

1. Ending First Minister Federalism

With our "federal" Constitution, Canada has two levels of government. Powers are divided between the government of Canada and the provincial governments, and there is some overlapping in such areas as agriculture, transport, health, and the environment, to mention just a few. As the size of government operations expanded during this century, and the range of government activities became more diversified, it made sense for officials from the two levels of government to coordinate their activities. Conflicts between two jurisdictions created tensions within Confederation, while overlapping or duplication created an unneeded cost for the taxpayers.

At first, federal-provincial conferences were rare. Through the 1960s and to the present day, however, they have grown in such number that on any given day some officials from both levels of government are meeting, and often several such gatherings are taking place simultaneously.

The pinnacle of this form of summit conference within Confederation occurs in the so-called First Ministers' Conferences, when the Prime Minister and premiers gather. These events have come to resemble a meeting of heads of state. Provincial premiers have many suggestions about how the government of Canada ought to run the country. They also want more powers and jurisdiction, and, invariably, more funding transferred to them from Ottawa.

These meetings have emerged as an unwritten part of our Constitution, as an unofficial institution for governing the country. First Ministers often can implement an agreement by using their party majority in their respective legislatures, shored up by the discipline of their party's whip. Especially with regard to constitutional matters, the whole process had become (until the October 26 referendum) like countries ratifying an international treaty that their governments have negotiated.

The working of First Minister federalism has been one of the causes for frustration in Canadian politics and among the Canadian people, since it effectively excludes the people and does not incorporate the methods of accountability you would normally expect to find in a democracy.

In the wake of the referendum on the Charlottetown Accord, on October 26, 1992, and the clear verdict from the

Canadian people that governments should stop tinkering with the Constitution, we can now "move ahead" by reverting to the practice of classical federalism. Provincial governments running provincial affairs according to their allocated powers under the Constitution, and the government of Canada addressing matters of concern to the whole country in keeping with the broader powers given to the national government under the Constitution, will be the new order of the day.

In this more disciplined framework, it will not be necessary for so much "conferencing" and the political posturing it too frequently generated. Coordination between different governments in Canada is important, but it will be far healthier for us as a country to deal with major political issues in Parliament and in the provincial legislatures where elected representatives, accountable to the people, can participate.

2. Providing for Referendums and Plebiscites

Thanks to the Charlottetown referendum, every Canadian is now familiar with the process of direct voting. We have had two other Canada-wide direct votes: on prohibition of alcohol in 1898, and on the issue of military conscription in 1942. There have also been some sixty provincial plebiscites, and several thousand at the municipal level. Some seventy-seven separate statutes in Canada give rise to the citizen's right to vote on certain issues or ballot questions.

In the three books I have written about referendums in Canada (*Lawmaking by the People*, *The People's Mandate*, and *Direct Democracy in Canada*), I have shown how this process of popular consultation on important issues is not some new-fangled idea, or some aberrant idea from the political fringes. Most of the statutes providing for referendums and plebiscites have been enacted by legislatures with Conservative or Liberal majorities. They began doing it a century ago.

As part of our democratic renewal, we must ensure that modern statutes are on the books in every Canadian electoral jurisdiction to permit citizens to play their role in the new partnership of decision-making. These useful democratic devices ought not to be relied upon only in times of crisis or when governments have their own backs to the wall. There is a constructive and positive role for direct voting, in limited but important ways, and a constructive attitude about such measures is an important element in the reformation of Canadian democracy.

3. Giving the People the Right of "Initiative"

Related to the direct democracy methods of plebiscites and referendums is the concept of "initiative." On the initiative of citizens themselves, a popular vote on a proposed law or important issue may be required. The initiative technique, which basically is triggered by a petition signed by a required minimum number of eligible voters, forms an integral part of the direct democracy component of participatory government.

Until recently in Canada, only municipal voting laws permitted the initiative to be used. It usually would be for votes on such matters as authorizing Sunday activities under the Lord's Day Act as happened in British Columbia, Alberta, Saskatchewan, Manitoba, Yukon, and the Northwest Territories. Other examples include votes to introduce fluoride into a municipality's water supply in Ontario, or votes on changing the ward basis for municipal elections, also in Ontario.

In 1988 I introduced legislation in the House of Commons to create the power of initiative for Canadian voters. Under my bill, entitled the Canada Referendum and Plebiscite Act, 10% of

Canadian electors "who are of the opinion that a question of national and public importance within the jurisdiction of Parliament should be submitted to a direct vote of the electors" could petition to have the vote held. The petition must include a concise statement of the question that is proposed to be submitted to the electors. Although I have kept this legislation continuously before Parliament since 1988, it has yet to be enacted into law.

Meanwhile, there is other activity in response to the clear desire for a hands-on democracy. In 1991, a new statute in Saskatchewan, the Referendum and Plebescite Act, created a power of initiative for provincial voters to bring an issue forward and require that a direct popular vote be held on it.

In British Columbia, as well, the provincial electorate in October 1991 voted overwhelmingly (74%) in support of this question: "Should voters be given the right, by legislation, to propose questions that the government of British Columbia must submit to voters by referendum?" A committee of the B.C. legislature is now studying how to implement this decision in law — which is not very hard, given we've had other statutes in the past that provided for direct voting.

This current resurgence of interest, particularly in western Canada, in the important power of citizens' initiatives is an encouraging sign of the renewal of democracy within our country.

4. Creating Ongoing Citizens' Forums

The Spicer Commission on Canadian unity, although a briefly lived extravaganza of popular consultation, did show the possibilities of grassroots discussion on important national issues. From the ground-level perspective of the community groups and individuals who participated, the commission was a success, and its central message was that people wanted to be better informed about public issues and to participate more effectively in public affairs.

One of the most moving public meetings I have ever attended was part of the Spicer Commission project. Members of my Etobicoke-Lakeshore riding association wanted to make a submission, obtained the forum questionnaire, and held several meetings to prepare carefully thought-out responses. Then we held a general meeting to discuss the group's draft.

In a school library that normally was large enough for such "policy" sessions, extra chairs had to be brought in and many people stood at the back and along the sides of the room. Everyone was a member of my party riding association, but not a single partisan word was spoken that evening. Men and women of all ages and racial backgrounds and religious faiths spoke with sharp differences in perspectives and conclusions regarding important questions for the future of Canada. It was clear that everyone cared very deeply about our country.

A sincerity and solemnity pervaded this session at John English School, Etobicoke, that evening. Although most members had worked with me over the seven years I had by then been their MP, it was the first time they were really sharing concerns, ideas, and dreams. In place of a "party-line" was a "plumb-line" — direct to people's genuine feelings.

Participants in this and other Spicer Commission meetings across the country were left with a refreshing belief in the value of a process where people can participate rather than be mere spectators. In a number of communities, policy discussion groups that initially formed in response to the commission continue to meet.

Recent developments in technology open new possibilities to inform citizens and provide communication, with our televisions and computers, in what might be called a "wired democracy." In the state of California, kiosks are available where citizens can call up on computers a wide range of current information about public issues and government programs and services. The government of Canada is working jointly with private communications companies here in our country, in what is called the Canarie Project, to open up an "electronic highway." Community libraries are an excellent location for these citizen computers.

5. Creating Regular Party Policy Conferences

Once upon a time, the party regulars were looked upon as the mainstay of our political system. Today they are too frequently bypassed. Opinion pollsters tell the party leaders directly what the people are thinking; no need to sound out the party rank and file. Fundraisers write letters directly to prospective contributors; or sometimes they invite people to purchase tickets for dinners at $500 or $1,000 a plate. Either way, the grassroots of the party tend to be left on the side in these arrangements.

Those in charge of policy formation have tended to see the party as just another constituency to be satisfied, or brought "onside," once a decision has already been made.

Policy conferences — where members of the party re-engage themselves with the Canadian people — are rare. Due to their infrequency, when they do take place the impulse is to try to cover all issues and broad themes. Significantly, political parties in recent years have started again to consult the grassroots in policy matters. Two years ago the Progressive Conservative Party went through an extensive process of drawing up policy from the grassroots, beginning with constituency meetings across the country, where ideas and proposals next moved up into regional conferences. These in turn led to province-wide policy conferences, and the gathering proposals from them

Listening to the People 73

culminated in a Canada-wide policy conference held in Toronto in August 1991.

Yet a fundamental gap remains between the policy development work that goes on within our parties, and the actions the government of the day actually takes. The party is in power in name only, not in reality. The process will continue to be disconnected and incoherent so long as there is no regular and systematic process for dealing with issues and policy questions in a way that is integral to the party and its leadership and direction. Without such a counter-balancing force within the party there will be no off-set to the preponderance of those who are really "in office" under the party's name: the opinion pollsters, the lobbyists, the special interest groups, the establishment members of the party itself, and the "permanent government" (the public servants). Yes, Minister!

6. Electing Cabinet Ministers by Caucus

Many people easily give voice to such sentiments as "we have to involve caucus more in setting the direction of the government," but their words ring empty because they do not propose a process by which this can happen. Prior to the 1984 general election, the PC caucus members met and adopted an agreement that, when in office, no legislation would go to Parliament unless it had first been approved by caucus. This was in fact, following 1984, frequently not done — and the role of caucus often amounted to being passively briefed on a measure immediately before it was presented in the Commons. When my father, Robert Boyer, was a member of the Ontario legislature under Premier Leslie Frost, the drill was clear and formal. A bill had to clear cabinet, then caucus, before it would be unveiled. If caucus members objected, the minister had to take it back to cabinet and revise it to solve the problems. This worked because there was a formal procedure that required an active role by caucus members.

While this approach must be carried through, I believe there is another procedure, far more significant, that should be implemented to ensure a central role for elected representatives, and to bring about a more effective and democratic partnership. One of the most effective ways to diffuse power, and make it more accountable to the people, would be to elect cabinet ministers by the caucus. Individual MPs in the government party caucus should elect from among themselves those who will serve as cabinet ministers, rather than having them handpicked by the Prime Minister.

In the legislature of the Northwest Territories, individual members elect from among themselves the government leader, and those who will hold cabinet portfolios. It is a selection process where the benefits of collective wisdom can be exercised, and where accountability and responsibility are diffused among elected representatives who in turn have to answer to their constituents for whoever is in cabinet and the decisions he or she may have taken.

In both Australia and New Zealand — the two other advanced democracies besides Canada to have adopted the British parliamentary system in its entirety — the sitting members of the Labour Party elect the members of their cabinet.

In the system that I am proposing, the Prime Minister would still allocate the portfolios among those chosen by caucus: if twenty MPs have been elected for twenty portfolios, the Prime Minister would decide which of them would be the best minister of finance, the best minister of agriculture, the best minister of defence, and so on.

The effects of this reform would be as refreshing as they would be dramatic. It would place a constraint on the extraordinary prime ministerial power in our existing Canadian parliamentary system, but it would at the same time free the Prime Minister from the pressures and obligations of deciding who should be in cabinet. It would empower Members of Parliament. It would establish a form of accountability and responsibility between backbenchers and cabinet ministers, something desperately needed since current practices and procedures in the House of Commons have totally eclipsed this accountability.

Here's how the process of cabinet election would work. A full caucus meeting held for the purpose of electing cabinet nominees would be informed by the Prime Minister of the exact number of portfolios to be filled. Next, any MPs not wishing to serve in cabinet would remove their names from the list. Balloting would then proceed to select, one by one, from among the remaining eligible and interested MPs, those who had majority caucus support to be in cabinet. Further rounds of balloting would continue to select those to be appointed parliamentary secretaries.

The process would be repeated annually, at the start of each summer. If caucus decided to replace two or three ministers by other MPs considered more capable or deserving, the Prime Minister would then reallocate portfolios well in advance of the resumption of parliamentary sittings in the autumn. This process would engender a fairly continuous fine-tuning of the cabinet, and avoid the gimmickry, expense, counterproductivity, and needless disruption of the infrequent major cabinet shuffle, much loved by the media as an event for speculation, but otherwise of no redeeming value.

Just as the Prime Minister would continue to have the right and power to designate which individuals (from among those elected by caucus) would hold particular portfolios, the Prime Minister would still have the right to remove any particular individual from his or her portfolio where circumstances warrant. In the event of a resignation or death, the caucus would elect one MP from among its number to fill the vacancy.

Caucus members wishing to advance to cabinet thus would have an incentive for maintaining effective and cordial communication with caucus colleagues, and for working hard to justify their eventual support for a cabinet position. Incumbent ministers under the existing system of prime ministerial appointment have little need for real contact with their fellow elected representatives of the people, certainly in comparison with time spent with government bureaucrats and special-interest-group representatives. These ministers, under this caucus election system, would discover a compelling new interest in remaining open and accessible to their colleagues in the backbenches.

This would realistically be a much healthier process. Rather than having to second guess and shadow box, MPs could play a more constructive role for all concerned since everyone would participate in collective decision-making regarding their shared success. Not only would this process engender more positive bonding between caucus members, its success would be based on the knowledge that MPs of the same political affiliation are like mountain climbers fastened together by the same rope: they get to the summit as one, or all tumble into the abyss together.

Since 1988 we Members of Parliament have elected our Speaker of the Commons. The success of that experiment ought to reassure that we can now move to the next stage in democratic reformation, the election by the people's elected representatives of cabinet, rather than their selection from on high by the Prime Minister.

7. Giving Parliament a Role in Making Appointments

No Canadian is unaware of allegations of patronage relating to government appointments.

Over our long history many have defended the present system of appointing people to public office.

They have argued, fairly soundly, that a party in power requires having people of its own orientation or persuasion in the various government offices where they can help implement and oversee the party's programs and policies.

Yet I believe there is a better way, one that will certainly remove the cloud of controversy from the process and ultimately enhance the credibility of public office holders in our country. A more public method of appointment is required. Parliament must be given a central role in the process.

Two recent developments show that this proposal is not so far-fetched, but is in fact a logical extension of a reform movement that has recently been advancing.

First, the appointment of judges by the government of Canada has been changed from the Byzantine practices of old, to a modern, truly revolutionary system: lawyers who want to become judges actually apply for the position. Forms are provided and are filled out by the applicant. A uniform system of screening and evaluating the applications is then carried out within the Department of Justice and by independent evaluation committees. The best person for the judgeship is then appointed. By extension, there is no reason why any Canadian citizen wishing to be appointed to any public office could not similarly make application and be assessed on his or her merits. It will be a happy day when we see the emergence of a "meritocracy" in our country.

The second development was the move by the Mulroney government to have certain cabinet-appointed public officials appear before a parliamentary committee prior to taking up their new duties. This has been the tentative beginning of a Canadian procedure that echoes the U.S. Congressional confirmation hearings, under which presidential appointees to cabinet and other positions are scrutinized and interrogated before they are confirmed as fit to hold the public office. We should not proceed down that road, for the process as developed by the Americans can discourage the recruitment of good people. Rather, we should involve elected representatives in reviewing and recommending for appointment by the government-qualified individuals from among the applicants. This would incorporate at an early stage the kind of public scrutiny so important in these matters.

This is one more way, as part of our hands-on approach to democratic renewal, that we can diffuse the power of the executive, rescue an important role for Parliament, ensure greater public accountability, and in the process provide a more equal opportunity for Canadians of merit to serve their country.

8. Sharing the Results of Opinion Polling

Supposedly, we know more about ourselves than ever before — thanks to the work of opinion pollsters. Business and service organizations retain pollsters to gain insight into public attitudes and markets. Governments and political parties are also major consumers of polling information. The trouble is, virtually all political party polling remains secret, and most government polling does, too, unless someone in the news media applies for it under the Access to Information Act.

So the curious result is that, while government appears to be listening to the people (or at least trying to figure out what the people think), the public itself is seldom let in on the secret.

In 1992 I presented a Private Member's Bill in Parliament that would require all government opinion polling results to be made public within fifteen days. It struck me as only fair that since public money is being spent to pay for these polls, since it is members of the public who are being asked the questions, and since the questions themselves presumably relate to public policy, the public ought to know the results. If governments are asking questions they would rather not share with the public, then that is all the more reason to require full and timely disclosure.

In Canadian public life today, the opinion pollster has risen to rare heights of prominence, somewhat like a high priest who can discern and interpret great truths. The pollster's work is no mere mathematical exercise, but, as Martin Goldfarb has explained, involves massaging and interpretation of the raw data. Since pollsters have now teamed up in business relationships with our major news media organizations, the Canadian public and their elected representatives alike are regularly presented by the media with fixed interpretations, based not only on what a representative sampling of Canadians have said but also on the subjective values or interests of the pollsters involved. Pollsters and the media exercise significant influence on the agenda which is followed in our country, and they are accordingly major players in the exercise of power and decision-making.

We are all free to ignore opinion polls if we choose, but there is no question that they have become a dominant and dominating aspect of our political landscape. So far as public policy is concerned, it will be at least one step forward to a healthier democracy to have the results of all government-sponsored polling shared with those who have a direct stake and necessary interest in the findings: the Canadian people.

9. Disclosing the Activities of Lobbyists

The past decade or two in Ottawa have seen the rise of major lobbying firms, organizations made up of Ottawa political and government insiders who insert themselves as middlemen between the public and the government (and extract substantial fees in the process).

Most people would argue that lobbying is inevitable, and some, mostly those in the trade itself, would even argue that it is desirable. Indeed, contemporary government depends on large volumes of information, giving lobbyists the additional role of coordinating and processing information germane to decision-making. The traditional insistence on secrecy in so many areas of government also contributes to the environment in which lobbyists thrive.

Accordingly, we can help ensure public confidence in government decision-making by requiring full disclosure of the activities of paid professional lobbyists.

Since elected representatives and public servants are subject to clear rules regarding conflict of interest, disclosure, and public accountability, it seems logical to require the same standards from those lobbyists who, in the words of one who appeared before a parliamentary committee in February 1993, have become "a part of government."

The Lobbyists Registration Act brought in by the Mulroney government in 1989 requires that lobbyists register and give a general indication of their intended activity. However, this system even falls short of the criteria mentioned by Prime Minister Mulroney himself in September 1985 when he called for legislation that would both "monitor and control" the activities of lobbyists in Ottawa. Nothing in the present system involves control in any form, and the monitoring is of a minimal level.

The legislation provided for a "comprehensive review" of the act's operation at the end of its first three years, and a parliamentary committee chaired by MP Felix Holtmann started this study early in 1993. A "comprehensive" approach certainly would involve looking at the work of lobbyists in greater detail, the nature of their relationship with their clients, and the nature of their relationship with government. In all three cases, the best and least costly way to achieve the needed restoration of balance and accountability in the exercise of power will be through much greater public disclosure.

This lobbyist registration legislation was a good first step, but now we must move on to the second generation of lobbyist legislation, to help create a hands-on democracy by allowing the public to understand more clearly how many vital decisions are being arrived at in nation's capital.

10. Ending Budget Secrecy and Closed Government

Government secrecy is a very big deal because, as they say, information is power. The more closely information is guarded within government, or stamped "top secret," the more powerful are those people who have access to it, and the weaker those who don't. Confidentiality is necessary, in some cases to protect national security, in other cases for the privacy of individual citizens, and in still other cases because of sensitive financial information. The Access to Information Act clearly lists various types of information that ought to be protected and kept secret, for common-sense reasons of good government.

Yet far too much of what is guarded under close secrecy is neither life threatening nor crucial to national security. For the sake of hands-on democracy, we need to pull away as many of the veils of secrecy as possible. Openness in government is a great cleansing agent, the best way to ensure that decisions are being properly taken.

The secrecy that especially surrounds budget-making in Canada is the ultimate form of this age-old practice, and it is increasingly harder to justify. Certainly Finance Minister Michael Wilson, and now Finance Minister Don Mazankowski, have engaged in a process of wide consultation prior to writing their budgets. Even so, there is still an unnecessary atmosphere of secrecy, and hence surprise, about government budgets. The finance minister unveils his proposals, and the elected representatives in his own party hear about them for the first time. Nevertheless, they are expected to stand and vote for them, under the discipline of the party whip.

11. REVAMPING PARLIAMENTARY VOTING

To free MPs for a more effective role in parliamentary proceedings, several changes can be made to permit "free votes" according to the individual MP's own conscience and informed views, and to wishes of constituents rather than an arbitrarily imposed "party line." This way elected representatives could be more attentive to the threefold nature of their responsibility: to constituents, conscience, and caucus.

The leaders of the parties, for their part, could formulate a governing doctrine: unity required in matters essential, diversity permitted in matters secondary. Once such a "doctrine of essential unity" is promulgated, and the party caucuses decide which issues are to be accorded primary and secondary status, a more robust democracy and more effective legislature would be free to emerge.

Internal and democratic reform of the House of Commons must therefore entail specific ways to overcome the constraining practices adopted by Canadian governments and caucus whips who enforce the party line and ensure that MPs are present in sufficient numbers to vote in support of the party position. This emphasis on voting together comes from the view, of course, that virtually every vote is a vote of confidence that, if lost by the government, could lead to an election. To remove the problem one must therefore also tackle the underlying concept of "confidence" votes.

An all-party Report on House of Commons Reform, from a committee chaired by Newfoundland MP James McGrath, recommended in 1985 that more free votes be permitted. The committee members sensibly suggested — in order to bypass the traditional view that every vote tests whether the government has the "confidence" of the Commons as reflected by its ability to win the numbers game — that any opposition motion intended to bring down a government would have to contain an explicit provision stating that its passage would constitute a vote of non-confidence. MPs would therefore vote on a measure, and it would be carried or defeated, according to their own views and the wishes of their constituents or region, as well as to whatever weight they chose to give to their party's official position on the matter. If the measure had not been made one of confidence, then it would meet its own fate, and the fate of the government would not be inextricably tied to it in a way that required a new election (or the possible formation of a new government in a house of minorities).

12. REQUIRING PARLIAMENTARY SCRUTINY OF OFF-BUDGET SPENDING

One of Parliament's most central roles is to authorize and review government spending. The procedures for doing this have long been established and in more recent times have been supplemented by the ongoing work of the Auditor General who reports directly to Parliament.

Yet there is one area of government spending that is not scrutinized by elected representatives in Parliament: the off-budget expenditures, or forgiveness of taxes, made by the cabinet under powers granted to it by the Financial Administration Act. Each year many millions of dollars, or the forgiveness of taxes or financial obligations worth many millions of dollars, are authorized in this way by cabinet (using something called a "remission order").

We can bring more accountability into this practice by setting up a more hands-on role for parliamentarians in their primary duty as financial watchdogs. Here's how. All of these off-budget expenditures must be made known to Parliament in advance, not to take effect for sixty days, until Parliament has either approved or rejected them. If Parliament does nothing by the end of sixty days, the cabinet-authorized expenditure automatically proceeds.

Three years ago I introduced legislation in the House of Commons to implement this procedure, in the form of amendments to the Financial Administration Act. I believe the amendment is a reasonable one, given the necessary balance between the government's interest in authorizing "remission orders" for this purpose, and the public and Parliament's interest in scrutinizing and authorizing these remission orders, which often involve many millions of dollars.

13. No More Royal Commissions

A longtime practice of governments in Canada, when confronted by a major question or difficult issue, has been to appoint a royal commission to study the matter. Once a royal commission is launched, it has a life of its own and ceases to exist only when it makes its final report.

Royal commissions are often very expensive. Just to mention a couple of many recent examples: $18-million was spent for the two-year Lortie Royal Commission on election finances, and $22-million for the Malouf Royal Commission on the sealing industry in Canada.

They also tend to go off into orbit. The extensive research, the public hearings, and the recommendations are generally completely divorced from the ongoing operations of Canadian government and politics. Once the report is made public, very few if any elected representatives have an "ownership" interest in it — one of the reasons so many reports end up collecting dust.

As part of our new hands-on democracy, parliamentarians themselves, as accountable public representatives, will deal directly with the major issues. Even if special research facilities and services are needed to carry out the work, it will be at a fraction of the expense associated with traditional royal commissions.

These thirteen specific steps for renewal are founded on an approach that says "trust the people." They are based on a belief in the collective wisdom of a well-informed public, and the importance, therefore, of ensuring that people are indeed informed and included. They offer a way to help rescue Parliament. They flow from the conviction that a healthy democracy ultimately depends on the consent of the governed.

CHAPTER SIX

The Politics of Engagement

Not all the changes flowing from what happened in Canada on October 26, 1992, were immediately obvious. That single referendum was itself just part of a much deeper reordering of our procedures of government and popular participation in decision-making. While it is difficult to describe all the features of a moving vehicle when you are inside, some observations about the transformation of Canadian democracy are already possible.

Participation Has Become a Defining Necessity

First, this reordering is more profound than a mere clash between "the elites" and "the people" as it was portrayed in many referendum post-mortems. We live in the age of telepolitics, and television loves confrontation because the nature of this picture-medium makes it the easiest to portray. Yet such an image of confrontation and contrast — and those who speak their briefly snatched words to reinforce the dramatic picture — is not our reality.

Many analysts of October 26, including those whose longer-worded commentaries appeared in print, were clearly influenced by this concept of confrontation between the classes in Canadian political society. The majority "No" vote in the referendum was held by many to be a slap at the elites of Canada and a repudiation of politicians. Yet what is to be made of the fact that many politicians themselves had responded to the emerging desire for direct participation by Canadian men and women in the process of constitution-making by creating the legal possibility of the referendum in the first place?

No reasoning politician who observed the aftermath of the Meech Lake Accord's demise in 1990, and who heard the earlier outcry from Canadians who had helplessly watched that ratification process unfold over three years, could remain immune to the democratic upsurge. People were rightly insisting on the need for government to obtain a popular mandate for any proposed constitutional changes.

At the pinnacle of the political elite, it was none other than Prime Minister Brian Mulroney who wrote into his government's throne speech of May 13, 1991, the intention to pass legislation that would permit the men and women of Canada to participate directly in that very process. It was Mulroney who said, on October 21, 1992, how he had changed his mind over the years regarding referendums. "I've come to recognize that in a modern, pluralistic society like ours, people do indeed require a much greater degree of participation . . . and that indeed there should be public consultation and the ultimate in that is a referendum." Politicians in Parliament duly enacted referendum legislation in June 1992. Politicians, the following September, duly passed the wording of the ballot question to be submitted to 18 million Canadian voters on October 26. Similarly, politicians in British Columbia and Alberta enacted laws in their legislatures requiring a referendum on any proposed constitutional changes. These laws required the people's mandate to be sought even before the legislature itself could consider the matter. By the same token, the referendum legislation was passed by politicians in Quebec. It required a popular consultation at the ballot box sometime in 1992, and this law flowed from the recommendations of the Boulanger-Campeau Committee, whose thirty-six members likewise represented the policy and political establishment of Quebec. This diverse group of members of Quebec's "elite" *all* called for a referendum.

Clearly, something deeper than a clash between the elites and the people had been at work in our country by the early 1990s, if not indeed earlier. This force had motivated many in leadership positions to understand that popular participation in making fundamental changes, such as to the Constitution, had become a necessity.

Perhaps it becomes easier to perceive something when it is expressed in reverse, or by its opposite. So think in this way about the question of whether to hold a national referendum. Just imagine the shrill outcry that would rightfully have been heard from Canadians living outside Quebec, British Columbia, and Alberta if they had not been able to vote on constitutional change, when their fellow citizens in those three provinces could. A Canada-wide referendum was utterly inevitable, in terms of practical political reality, even though a number of other senior political representatives (most notably Constitutional Affairs Minister Joe Clark) held out against it past the eleventh hour.

Canada's politicians and so-called elites were, in fact, as divided as the people themselves over whether direct democracy has a role in settling our country's affairs. I encountered voters during the campaign who said, "You politicians should decide this. That's what we elect you for." Yet vastly more welcomed the opportunity to vote on the accord. They acted as if this was the most natural thing in the world, and took their democratic responsibility seriously.

POLITICS IN THE AGE OF DISBELIEF

Something deeper has also been stirring in the attitudes of people who have grown sceptical.

The referendum was inevitable not only at the level of practical political necessity to avoid a patchwork result as several provinces voted on the issue, at different times, with differently worded ballot questions, following different campaigns, while other provinces retained the decision in their legislatures. This potential for confusion alone certainly helped produce the political dynamic leading to a single Canada-wide vote held on the same day.

On a more profound level, however, we can see, as a second major observation, that the inevitability of the 1992 referendum came from a democratic transformation that has been working through societies around the world.

Through all levels of contemporary society — from prime ministers to parents, religious leaders, employers, teachers, elected representatives, doctors, custodians of orphanages, and police — virtually anyone in a position of trust is viewed with suspicion. We are witnessing profound scepticism in all authority. Our present times could be called the Age of Disbelief.

This is not necessarily bad. It did not surprise me when, as our country's political leaders held up the Charlottetown Accord and told people what it meant, dubious Canadians demanded to see the legal text. Many did not really want to read the boring details any more than they relish the idea of ploughing through the technical instructions to their VCR. They were simply saying, "Prove it." Asking to see the "fine print" is a theme song in the Age of Disbelief.

For several reasons, loss of credibility has been accelerating in recent decades. It began moving into overdrive with the collapse of communist regimes and the end of the Cold War, which removed even more of the top-heavy restraints on human societies, both in central and eastern Europe as well as in our Western industrial democracies.

So we return again to this concept of a cultural re-confederation of Canada. The "reality check" with Canadians conducted on October 26 refocused the image of who we are as a people and what we are as a country. Joe Clark, in a 1991 Canada Day address, said that quite apart from the worry over Quebec's separation, his concern was that Canada may be separating "from its own modern reality." Part of the explanation, he told his Toronto audience, is that we do not realize what we have become. "We have based our assumptions about Canada on facts which have changed. Our country has changed, but our vision of it hasn't and often our institutions haven't either." Conversely, the referendum on October 26 showed that assumptions which governments and political leaders made about our country, the nature of the issues before us, and the best way to address those issues, may all have been based on a vision that itself, ironically, had separated from the realities of Canada.

It is as if a Canadian portrait had been painted that day of October 26, with each voter making a single brush stroke in the composite rendition of ourselves. The portrait shows strength of character as well as all our wrinkles and warts. Many self-reassessments have been possible since that date because the verdict revealed truths about our country, and re-expressed some of our hard-edged Canadian realities, in ways never so effectively projected by opinion polls or public commentaries.

Nor did these truths ever really register with many, or become understood, when conveyed only through speeches and academic analysis. Nothing else, it is now clear, could have spoken with the same brisk eloquence as a collective statement rendered at the ballot box following a process of debate and deliberation. We had already learned this, of course, but the point was only dimly remembered from earlier Canadian history. Now this lesson again is within the ken of every Canadian's immediate and personal experience. To understand our democracy we must not just read about it in history books; we have to live it.

LESSONS OF THE OCTOBER 26 REFERENDUM

There was indeed something wholesome and cathartic about the referendum and its outcome. Even many of us who enthusiastically supported the Charlottetown Accord and campaigned for it felt no deep sense of shock or dismay at the outcome — indeed, perhaps we felt a measure of relief. The new approach, so necessary to take, would now be easier.

The Charlottetown Accord smashed into a pretty solid wall of opposition on October 26. Among the rubble it was possible to discern that the approach to constitution-making of recent years — one of trying to combine more and more major political issues into a single, comprehensive package — was now dead.

Since 1867 constitution-amending had mostly been specific and clearly directed to an identifiable purpose. This conservative, incrementalist approach had been displaced, however, under Prime Minister Pierre Trudeau. His scheme was to make wholesale and wide-ranging amendments, not to fine-tune the

Constitution but to radically alter its character, as with provisions to define and entrench all our political rights and freedoms within the Constitution, and to seek to entrench the "economic union" within the Constitution as well.

Even when attempted by Trudeau, this approach of negotiating far-reaching and comprehensive amendments had obvious flaws and failures. He had to jettison the economic union provisions completely in face of opposition from provincial premiers. He succeeded in having a Charter of Rights entrenched only when it included a "notwithstanding" clause that permitted legislatures to set aside constitutional rights in specific cases. To win patriation, he negotiated an amending formula that imposed a unanimity straitjacket on many subsequent amendments. Most seriously, Trudeau only achieved even these amendments with the exclusion of Quebec, thereby leaving fully one-quarter of the Canadian people in many respects outside the new constitutional regime.

Once this First Minister federalism got going, it seemed no one could stop it. Under Prime Minister Mulroney, the next round of large-scale constitution-amending continued, in spite of lessons evident in the lacerating failures of Trudeau's much trumpeted constitutional "success." The Meech Lake Accord was the further product of this process.

The five requirements of Quebec, as identified in 1985 by Premier Robert Bourassa, had been augmented in rounds of negotiation with the other provincial premiers, who predictably added a few more points of their own. This same approach failed to produce a constitutional amendment, however, after three years of attempted ratification, thanks to the amending formula the Trudeau round had bequeathed us. This made it even harder to deal with all the other unfinished business Trudeau had left behind after his fourteen years in office. We could still hear the taunting echo of his 1980 commitment to constitutional "renewal of federalism," solemnly pledged but noticeably unfulfilled. It would normally have been clear, by June 1990, that the time had come to seek a solution by other means. However, this was not to be.

The mood of disappointment and rejection within Quebec, in the wake of the Meech Lake Accord's demise, led to an act being passed in the National Assembly requiring that either in the spring or fall of 1992 a referendum be held on sovereignty. Anticipating the peril in such a vote, Prime Minister Mulroney sought to soften the risk by attempting, yet again, a series of constitutional amendments that would renew Confederation. The result: the Charlottetown Accord. It combined, by far, the most numerous and far-reaching package of constitutional changes ever proposed in a single stroke since Confederation. This was going for broke. This was the comprehensive approach pushed to the limit.

Many times during the referendum campaign I said of the Charlottetown Accord, "This is as good as it gets." I was referring to any negotiated agreement trying to resolve at one time all the major constitutional issues of the past decade in a well-connected and honourable compromise. Given the interests that had been expressed by various groups and regions, and in light of all the divergent issues and proposals needing to be reconciled, it simply could not be done, in my view, any better than what we found negotiated in the Charlottetown Accord. Yet a crucial point must be stressed here: this accord was "as good as it could get" within the approach of including all the issues in a package of constitutional amendments.

What crashed on October 26 was that all-in approach. Nothing more; nothing less.

As a result, two new lessons have been taught by Canadians about our method of government.

The first lesson: *No more comprehensive constitutional amendments.* In the future, we will revert to the more conservative or incrementalist approach to constitution-making. We will deal only with one issue or problem at a time, and be very specific about the proposed change and its consequences. We will leave the Constitution alone, and only seek to amend it when absolutely necessary. The new principle will be: that which it is not necessary to amend, it is necessary not to amend. Issues that have been "constitutionalized" over the past decade can once again be dealt with in Parliament and the legislatures, one by one, in a more open and accessible forum where the participants are directly accountable.

The second lesson: *No proposed constitutional change can ever again be implemented in Canada without referral first to the people in a direct vote.* Since it became clear that the best and the brightest in our policy and political establishment could not sell the Charlottetown Accord to a majority of Canadians, a new presumption has now been raised: that a proposed change in our Constitution does not have popular support unless it can be clearly demonstrated that it has.

Almost by accident we now have developed a constitutional custom or convention that, in its effect, is the same as the clear wording contained in the Australian Constitution, which requires a referendum to ratify any constitutional change. In our country, what the Beaudoin-Edwards Committee was too timid to recommend in 1990, in terms of obligatory referendums to ratify constitutional proposals, the people have themselves provided, both through their demand over the past few years for a say in constitutional change, and in the results of October 26 itself.

The End of the Constituent Assembly Idea

The concept of a constituent assembly was proposed by opponents of the Meech Lake Accord during the time that constitutional agreement was undergoing its three-year ratification process, and was raised again by even more proponents of far-reaching constitutional change in the discussions leading to the Charlottetown Accord in 1992. This idea also became a victim of the October 26 referendum. Certainly no obvious future awaits a constituent assembly in Canada, essentially for three reasons.

First, a constituent assembly, made up of delegates selected from across the country, would presumably be called into existence only to deal with a fundamental rethinking of our constitutional arrangements. It is really not conceivable that it would be convened for deliberations on a single, technical, and specific amendment to the existing Constitution. Yet the political message from the Canadian voters, as now interpreted by our country's politicians and government leaders, is precisely that there be no more all-in approach to constitution-making. "Hands-off" the Constitution means hands-off for everybody.

Second, any constituent assembly seeking to redefine fundamental Canadian arrangements in constitutional terms would have to grapple with all the same issues that were considered by the political leaders and government officials who brought us such documents as the Meech Lake and Charlottetown accords. In other words, we could change the players who move the pieces on the board, but the same bishops, knights, rooks, castles, queens, and pawns are in play, and given the rules of the Canadian political chess game, they have to be moved within fairly clear and predetermined patterns.

Indeed, October 26 taught us just how narrow the tolerances are for some of these moves or changes. Simply because it would be a constituent assembly of regular Canadians, they would, being Canadians, have to deal with all the same problems we have lived so long with that we seem unable to do without: the Senate, Quebec's relationships within Canada, our ethnic and linguistic diversity, the overlapping structures of a federal state, the nature of the Supreme Court, the position and power of aboriginal peoples within Canada, the difficulty of reconciling equality of provinces, the equality of citizens, and the equality of two founding linguistic groups, and so on through the long litany of Canada's defining arrangements and relationships.

Dealing instead with our major political issues one at a time, and outside the Constitution, points to a revised and more relevant role for Parliament and the legislatures. This is the third reason a constituent assembly has no future in Canada. Canada already has a constituent assembly to which men and women of Canada are elected in a free and democratic choice of the people at regular intervals to consider the public business. That assembly is called Parliament.

Indeed, if a constituent assembly is intended to be a deliberative body made up of individuals representing all the constituencies or elements within Canada, it is impossible to conceive of a more accurate reflection of our society than one finds, at any given interval, in the 295 members elected to the Canadian House of Commons. All regions of the country are represented, both sexes are present, and MPs are individuals of different ethnic, religious, and national backgrounds, able to speak many different languages, to practice a variety of professions, to work in a number of trades, to recount a world of different life experiences, to express philosophies and points of view ranging all across the political spectrum, and to speak for the elites and the underdogs because of their own personal stations in life.

How could a constituent assembly be more representative? How could it acquire the informed view and political understanding of the country that it would need to develop policies more realistic than those which existing Members of Parliament, daily accountable to their electorate, can fashion? If a constituent assembly was chosen only from Canada's so-called elites, who would represent the rest of our people? If it was selected, alternatively, only from "ordinary" Canadians, who would bring to bear the practical understanding from experience of how our institutions interact and our political life functions?

At a conference on constitution-making at the University of Ottawa, April 1990, I observed that it really matters little whether constitutional proposals are developed by First Ministers, by Parliament, or by a constituent assembly, provided that once the best and brightest people available have produced the document they consider to be the finest possible arrangement, it is submitted directly to Canadians for ratification or rejection in a referendum. In one sense, the greatest constituent assembly of all consists of our single country with its 18 million voters, who deliberate on proposals and then collectively render their verdict. The other constituent assembly is Parliament. Anything in between is an unsatisfactory halfway house.

DIRECT VOTING CAN ENHANCE EXISTING PROCEDURES

The idea of involving the people through direct voting is not to displace our existing parliamentary procedures or the role of elected representatives, but to enhance them through the additional participation from time to time of all Canadian citizens in deciding the fundamental questions concerning our country's future. The process envisaged here would complement, not compete with, parliamentary democracy.

Some critics of referendums and plebiscites allege that procedures for full citizen participation are incompatible with our system of government.

However, Canada and other countries have had considerable experience with these devices of direct democracy. Our Canada-wide plebiscites would have been ever more numerous had Prime Minister Robert Borden got his way in 1914 for a plebiscite on senate reform, or Wilfrid Laurier in 1917 on conscription, or even Pierre Trudeau in the early 1980s on the Constitution. The provincial plebiscites and referendums include many that are recent: October 1991 in Saskatchewan, October 1991 in British Columbia, and May 1992 in Northwest Territories. In the last round of municipal elections, more plebiscites were added to the list of several thousand direct votes at the local level.

Besides our Canadian experience, other parliamentary democracies of the Westminster model have combined direct democracy with representative democracy. In Great Britain, for instance, a country-wide plebiscite in 1975 asked citizens to vote directly on whether they wanted their country to continue its membership in the European Common Market. On two other occasions in the 1970s, referendums were held in Britain relating to devolution (a mild form of "sovereignty-association") for Scotland and Northern Ireland.

An even better example is provided by Australia, since that country is so similar to Canada. We both have a federal system of government, and are constitutional monarchies operating with a parliamentary system of government. In 1900 the Australians decided that any constitutional amendment would have to be ratified by the people. They added a provision to their Constitution expressly requiring popular ratification. As a result, on thirty-two occasions during this century, when someone came up with a new idea to change the Constitution, the proposal was submitted to Australian citizens to express their verdict at the ballot box. On eight occasions a majority of the people were persuaded that the proposal was good and voted to ratify it; on all the other occasions they defeated the proposal. That is exactly how a democracy should work. If you cannot persuade a majority of the people to make a change in their country's Constitution, you have no business — legally or morally — changing it.

A Transition from Spectators to Participants

The referendum process changes Canadians from spectators into participants. Many people have lamented that in contemporary Canada individuals are quick to assert their rights but slow to take up their responsibilities. They want to see equal emphasis placed on the duty of citizens.

In reality, however, most Canadians are preoccupied with many demands on their time. Lack of interest over recent years in constitutional proposals, for example, may not only have been attributable to many Canadians' bleak sense of déjà vu on this topic. Most of us do, after all, have more immediate human preoccupations of an economic and social nature. This produces the phenomenon of "intelligent ignorance." A busy Canadian might understandably have chosen to ignore constitutional proposals, perceiving them to be academic and that the time and effort to learn about them would be wasted. Why study for an exam if nobody is going to ask you the questions? Yet if there is going to be an exam, if you are going to be handed a ballot paper and asked to mark your choice on a major Canadian issue, a new imperative suddenly enters the picture. A valid reason now exists for paying attention.

How this process works was shown in 1988 in Prince Edward Island. For years, even before Confederation, politicians, engineers, and promoters had spoken about tunnels, bridges, causeways, and ferry boats between the mainland and the island. In the election campaign of 1962, national Liberal Party leader Lester Pearson promised a causeway. Yet only in 1988 did Premier Joe Ghiz actually put the question directly to the Islanders in a plebiscite, asking whether they favoured a fixed-link connection to the mainland. I saw how, for the first time ever, Islanders could focus on their future and define what the island meant to them, because each of them had to vote on the issue. That process, and the deadline for a decision, forced a concentrated debate involving economic benefits, tourism impacts, environmental concerns, and "the Island way of life." The spectators had become participants — not a bad exercise to go through.

Similarly, the politics of engagement has worked its beneficial transforming effects on Canadians in many direct votes. Quebecers approaching the May 20, 1980, referendum on sovereignty-association, for example, were forced to face the difficult question of whether they wanted an independent Quebec or a Quebec within a greater Canada. The debate was intense, because the issue raised by the separatists was fundamental and emotional. There was no escaping the fact that the process would be cathartic. Yet at the end of the campaign, the issue had been fully and fairly examined from all sides, and each Quebecer could express his or her personal verdict at the ballot box.

If we want to call ourselves a democracy, we must not be afraid to use democratic procedures.

The Constitutional Fiction of Electoral Mandates

To a great degree, modern Canadian elections are about people and personalities as much as they are about policy. Numerous policy issues and proposals are mixed into the course of a single general election, and from that process it is impossible to extract a specific mandate for a particular course of action.

Our constitutional doctrine about a government having a "mandate" actually means only that is has majority support in the House of Commons. However, this has been too generously interpreted in Canada as meaning that the government has a blank cheque to govern as it sees fit, provided it can keep its majority in the Commons.

This constitutional fiction is handy for the routine daily operation of Parliament and the government of Canada, but it should never be stretched so far as to provide justification for transforming measures that were never debated or contemplated in the preceding election campaign. The danger in repeatedly doing so can be accurately measured in the current levels of political discontent and disillusionment across our country.

Another fiction is that parliamentarians understand the issues but the people do not. Some of my colleagues in Parliament, a great many senior civil servants, some academics, a few journalists, and a number of my constituents allege that the Canadian people cannot be trusted to deal with important public issues because they are not adequately informed about the implications. This is a bit like the pot calling the kettle black.

Dr. Jim Henderson, an Ontario MPP who is a critic of the shortcomings of our Canadian legislative assemblies, has pointed out that the private member technically has the potential to influence decisions. Yet a network of traditions has developed in most legislatures that pulls in the opposite direction: members almost always vote as their parties instruct them. Thus, Henderson also observed, "once a newly elected member has learned this lesson, some of them easily and understandably lose interest in always knowing what a particular vote is all about."

Often MPs vote on legislation without being adequately informed about all of its implications. I know I have. In some cases, members do not even know what bill they are voting on but simply vote with their party when their turn comes. A couple of months ago in the midst of a vote, I asked the cabinet minister sitting in front of me if he realized what he had just voted for.

"No, what?" he asked.

"You just voted to cut your salary by fifteen percent!"

The system we have today is the end-product of insipid parliamentary democracy.

THE POLITICS OF ENGAGEMENT

A democracy is governed ultimately by consent of the governed rather than by their coercion. Governing against the value system of a society only creates long-term difficulties.

The idea I am advancing is a "politics of engagement" — where the Canadian people themselves are engaged in both the risk and the consequences of deciding issues. This applies not only in government, but in industry and education, in environmental issues from east coast fisheries to west coast logging, and in personal, family, and community life as well.

The Canadian experience with direct democracy, like any tapestry threaded together after the fact from various strands of historical events, shows a wide array of colours. Some are most pleasing to the eye, others less so. Yet, together they form a whole and should be judged in their entirety and in their context. One thing this tapestry shows is that direct democracy in Canada has been about the politics of engagement.

The politics of engagement means that, in public policy and decision-making in government, all analysis and action proceeds on the understanding that genuine democracy involves a partnership. The partnership is between those who wield power — whether they be parents, bosses, judges, public servants, union leaders, bankers, police, cabinet ministers, military officers, or elected representatives — and those who live with the consequences of how that power is exercised.

The central value in this partnership is to achieve the greatest good for the greatest number, and that good can best be identified by the active involvement of all concerned. It is not a selfish exercise of power of a self-aggrandizing process, but an altruistic one. The lessons of history are harsh, and this century has contributed many horrific examples of self-aggrandizing powermongers: Hitler, Stalin, Pol Pot, Idi Amin, the bosses of organized crime and corrupt unions, merciless "captains of industry," corrupt leaders of religious organizations. The lesson is clear: Human nature requires that power be diffused, not concentrated. A second lesson is this: There must be accountability in the exercise of power.

If the object is to diffuse power, and to ensure true accountability, what better way than by ensuring that it is shared with those whose existence gives the power-holders their meaning in the first place? The way to bring about this sharing is the politics of engagement. As discussed above, one of the many methods of engaging the people in the risk of decision-making and the obligation to live with the joint decision is of course direct democracy.

The illusion has been that the strength of a country lies in its leaders. The reality is that it resides in its people. The crucial truth is that the people and the leaders need one another, and that this relationship, this partnership, is central to a healthy democratic society. Too much history has been written from the perspective of kings and emperors and presidents and prime ministers. The ideal that forms the core of our democracy is more than trust in the people by those who are in government, although that is itself vital. Trust by the people in our system of government and in its elected representatives is the nobler vision, although even this is still not enough. *Mutual trust is the ideal for a democracy.* The truly important next step is to recreate a healthy relationship between the leaders and the people, since each depends on the other.

CHAPTER SEVEN

Democratic Conservatism

OUR POLITICAL PARTIES are unique national institutions. At one and the same time they are moulded by the country and all its diversities, yet in turn seek to shape and direct the same country that gives rise to them in the first place. It is a symbiotic relationship, a permanent union between two entities, each of which depends for its existence on the other. For all their shortcomings, our parties are essential to the operation of Canadian political society and the functioning of Parliament.

Most Canadians probably accept that our political parties come as a mixed blessing. First, on the positive side, a political party provides a vehicle for getting and controlling political power on a sustained basis. This in turn provides direct control of the apparatus of government, and stability, some predictability, and certain accountability in the political system.

For example, when Sir John A. Macdonald helped nurture the Conservative Party into existence in the mid-1800s, groupings of like-minded and common-interest individuals began forming for concerted action. This meant that, through the Conservative Party and its control of government and Parliament, the political ideas of Macdonald and other

Confederation Conservatives on such topics as industry, the economy, and society could be expressed in tangible ways: longer railways, higher tariffs, fairer factory conditions, an expanded franchise, a codified criminal law.

Ever since those days, political parties have campaigned on policy platforms, and the electorate had choices that would not have been available to it in the absence of political parties.

Yet there has also been a negative side. The invention of the political party in Canada also brought with it two drawbacks: the risk that political corruption would be organized in a systemic way, and a tension between the political principles of individuals and the pragmatic demands of the party organization.

"PLEDGES FIRST, PRINCIPLES AFTERWARDS"

Today our parties in Canada are in a new historical phase. Respect for them appears to be at an all-time low. My own review of party election platforms and subsequent performance in office suggests that parties which have formed governments in Canada in recent decades have been far more willing to deviate from their election pledges — often indeed to completely reverse themselves — than parties were before the 1960s.

In the 1988 general election, for instance, the Mulroney government campaigned on the very specific proposal to acquire nuclear-propelled submarines for the Canadian Armed Forces, outlining the role such vessels would perform and their estimated cost. During the election, Mulroney as party leader explicitly reiterated, in response to specific questions from the news media, that acquisition of the subs remained a policy of his government. Since the Mulroney government was re-elected, one could reasonably claim that it then had a mandate to proceed with this program. In fact, it cancelled the submarine acquisition plan shortly after the election.

Such reversals seem to have happened after most of the Canadian general elections of recent times. In 1974, for example, Liberal leader Pierre Trudeau made a popular election commitment to "double track" the railroad from the prairies to the west coast in order to accommodate faster transportation of wheat to the sea ports. The promise, however, was dropped quietly when the finance minister announced that funds for the project were not available. The railroad plan was cancelled, even though, according to our election doctrines, it had been mandated by the people.

Another reversal occurred after the 1974 election, in which PC leader Robert Stanfield pledged that if elected he would impose price and wage controls to curb inflation. Liberal leader Trudeau ridiculed the idea ("Zap — you're frozen!"), and it was clearly not Liberal policy. When the Liberals won the election and received their mandate to govern, however, Prime Minister Trudeau proceeded to impose the selfsame controls that, arguably, the electorate had expressly rejected.

A decade earlier, Liberal leader Lester Pearson's promise to build a causeway to Prince Edward Island met the identical post-election fate of Trudeau's second track of rails. Trudeau in earlier days had himself been outraged by Prime Minister Pearson and the Liberal Party's breathtaking flip-flop on nuclear weapons for the Bomarc missiles that led to a major national debate, in 1963, about nuclear arms and Canadian independence from American political control.

Even the New Democratic Party, which has sometimes sounded sanctimonious in describing itself as a "party of principle," has shown in office that, just like the other brokerage political parties, it too could autonomously change its electoral mandate. A recent example is the Ontario NDP government under Bob Rae. The NDP had campaigned vigorously for a state-operated automobile insurance plan as a matter of party principle, but announced a year after the election that this fundamental commitment would have to be "postponed." They also switched their position on Sunday shopping, reversed their stated views on gambling casinos, and turned around their policy on deficit financing.

This behaviour by parties shows why the constitutional fiction that an electoral mandate settles specific issues has become a dangerous doctrine in the context of Canadian brokerage party politics. It also helps account for the levels of public anger with politicians, the public's mistrust of the intentions of government, and the significant decline in the number of Canadians with fixed allegiances to political parties.

Powerful governments have long promoted a doctrine of parliamentary democracy that brazenly holds that once elected by virtue of winning the most seats in a general election, regardless of the size of their party's popular vote, they have a mandate to deal with any issue that comes up during the life of that Parliament. Most political scientists and media commentators operate within this accepted view, and have, along with many compliant politicians, reinforced its popularity by their teachings, commentaries, and behaviour.

Yet to assert that a government can go to war, amend the country's constitution, or reverse a whole pattern of trade policies or immigration programs, when such courses of action had not even been talked about in the election from which it received its "mandate," is to stretch a doctrine further than is reasonable in a democracy.

Governments most assuredly are elected to govern. However, the defiant government that says, regarding an issue of transcending importance that was never even broached in the previous election, "We can do this because we have a mandate to govern," is making as extreme a distortion of things as was made in the assertion after the 1988 general election that because 57% of voters had voted other than Tory, a majority of Canadians had voted against the Free Trade Agreement for which the Tories had campaigned and, therefore, government members had no mandate to vote in Parliament to ratify the agreement. Both these extremes display a certain silliness. It is no wonder that Canadians, faced with such assertions, may be uncertain of exactly what they have decided, as far as specific issues go, in a general election.

The brokerage role of Canadian political parties has been viewed, if not with enthusiasm, at least with tolerant understanding by those who recognize the integrative function parties perform in putting together coalitions in which all the diverse forces of such a country can be represented. "National unity is preserved," argued political historian Frank Underhill, "by having every interest-group effectively inside the party which controls the government." Brokerage politicians, suggests University of Toronto political theorist H.D. Forbes, "put party loyalty ahead of doctrinal purity or devotion to abstract principles." He believes that Stephen Leacock admirably caught the spirit of brokerage politics when he said, "Pledges first, principles afterwards."

Brokerage parties and the old brokerage theory of Canadian politics that viewed the process with approbation may, Forbes thinks, "be parts of an ideological apparatus for suppressing consideration of issues that would threaten the dominant classes in modern society."

Even the New Democratic Party, which has presented itself as the socialist alternative, has increasingly been co-opted into the system of brokerage politics, softening its doctrine, developing election platforms based on opinion polling as is done by the Progressive Conservatives and the Liberals, and moderating its positions as it seeks greater support in the so-called political mainstream. As socialists, they have become "backsliders." Moreover, the debt crisis is now making "conservatives" of Canada's socialist parties in office, just as it did with the Labour Party in New Zealand, which radically cut government spending, eliminated operations, and privatized many functions. The process has gathered such momentum that one can quip, is anyone left on the left?

It is important to understand these broader political tendencies in Canadian politics, in order to grasp the true basis for the political reorientation now under way in our country. Whatever the long-term prospects may be for such political formations as the Reform Party of Preston Manning, the National Party of Mel Hurtig, the Confederation of Regions (COR) Party in New Brunswick, or the Bloc Québécois of Lucien Bouchard, they are all evidence of instability and transition in contemporary Canadian political parties.

THE ARRIVAL OF DEMOCRATIC CONSERVATISM

It is in this context that I believe Canadian political conservatism, generally but not exclusively to be found within the confines of the Progressive Conservative Party of Canada, is now evolving to a new stage. I believe this next stage in its long evolution may best be described as "democratic conservatism."

Democratic conservatism represents a fusion or integration of broadly defined conservative values with a thoroughgoing democratic approach.

These conservative values include, for me at least, the following: recognition of the spiritual nature of our existence, acceptance of an integral role for humans within the ecological system, conservation of the natural environment, respect for the many strands in our richly diverse Canadian cultural inheritance, the primacy of family and local community, a sense of duty to serve the country, the feeling of personal obligation to our fellow citizens, voluntarism, respect for time-tested Canadian traditions, acceptance of the formative and controlling role of institutions within society, the valuable efficiency of a market economy, the need to uphold law and maintain social order, the importance of self-reliance, the need for privacy of the individual, the understanding that government ought to work in partnership with the people, and the belief that we can improve our lot more through cultural values than through government actions.

When I speak of these conservative values being integrated with a more democratic approach, I am suggesting the need for less top-down, or elite, or father-knows-best approach in Canadian politics and government. What we now need, to repeat a point made earlier in this book, is a new partnership.

A democratic society is defined more by how decisions are made, how people participate in the decision-making process, and how mandates for an agreed-upon course of action are achieved — rather than by any effort to obliterate natural distinctions and hierarchies based on talent, merit, wealth, education, or cultural heritage. I believe in making Canadian society democratic, not in levelling it.

A democratic country is one in which everyone is not the same. Especially in Canada with our rich diversities of language, cultures, and regions, a democratic approach is absolutely essential. Because of our great diversity, the *process* by which a decision is reached can be as important, and is often more significant, than the decision itself. We Canadians have no choice but to be democrats.

INTERNALIZING OUR RESPONSIBILITY

A *democratic* process that truly engages Canadians is central to the success of these conservative values being reflected in the way the Conservative Party operates in government and the way it offers true choices to Canadians. That is vital, in turn, because we genuinely need to engage ourselves in coming to grips with this country's political agenda.

It has long been a curious mutation of our colonial mentality that we *externalize* responsibility, rather than turning with maturity into ourselves. Since the 1960s Quebecers have shown the way, seeking to be "maitre chez nous" (masters of our own house), and with this mentality developing a political culture where the soul truly is nourished and political activity is both germane and authentic.

Yet in the rest of Canada we flounder because of a destructive frame of mind, weighed down by an attitude that charges with frustration and, like lightning, strikes the highest and most visible target — usually the Prime Minister of the day — with bolts of blame. For all their human frailties, our prime ministers have contended well with the challenges generated by the circumstances of their times.

Canadian historian Frank Underhill once told me that "a great leader should be a one-man distillation of the country." I suspect, though, that there is always a long time between great leaders, and what are we to do in the meantime? Are we to wait for the great leader, the one who, as Norman Mailer suggests, takes "national anxieties so long buried and releases them to the surface where they belong"? Or, is there another way, one that we are groping toward but have not yet fully recognized?

Isn't the new image of democracy in Canada one in which greater popular participation is understood as being vital to our national well-being? Does personal involvement not become necessary in a country where the duties and responsibilities, as well as the "rights," of each citizen are being emphasized?

Making real connections, rather than simply talking past one another as we so often do in personal life and certainly in our party-dominated public "debate," is crucial to overcoming the banality that pervades much of our public life. An inhibition that it would be unseemly to act too often has restrained us from robustly embracing our authentic Canadian reality. The body moves, but the soul within it languishes, ignored and undernourished.

We Canadians have been strangely fugitive from our own reality and have engaged in massive conspiracies to bury our past and hide from our history. Emotionally, we even hide from one another, and from ourselves. We're deep inside the shell.

Apart from the dwarfing vastness of our land and our inherited colonial preference for getting the answer from elsewhere, our political structures and practices of governance have also been partly responsible for this lack of sharing. Yet now in the mid-1990s we come to an historic period in our evolution as a country: we are finally facing up to the conflict between the political and cultural ideas of Canada as a nation.

A COHERENT PATTERN OF THINKING WITHIN THE CONSERVATIVE PARTY

The Progressive Conservative Party as one of our country's long-enduring institutions on the political landscape likewise is coming to grips with this moment of history. As I noted earlier, our political parties mirror the nation, so it follows that the democratic resurgence within the country should also seek to be expressed in terms of democratic renewal within the parties. This renewal is based on ideas and values and policies that can now be brought together in a coherent pattern.

Earlier this year I published a booklet, *Democratic Conservatism*, outlining the evolution of Canadian political conservatism from colonial times to the present day. It was necessary background in order to make sense of the different values now found within the contemporary Conservative Party. It is also helpful, in charting the course ahead, to know where we have been in the past.

To date, there have been five distinctly different phases in the evolution of the ideas and values of Conservatives in Canada: (1) *colonial conservatism*, which was supplanted by (2) *confederation conservatism*, to which was added (3) *public interest conservatism* early in the twentieth century, followed by (4) *social conservatism* arising out of the Depression and wartime conditions, and then (5) *enterprise conservatism* from the mid-1960s to the present.

There is not enough space here to summarize the principal ideas and conservative values associated with each of these phases. Yet one important observation about the evolution of Canadian political conservatism is that the attitudes and ideas of one era do linger on, their intellectual imprint evident on subsequent generations who inherit the conservative tradition. For this reason, moving forward to democratic conservatism at this stage does not represent a break with the past, or a repudiation of earlier conservative thinking, but represents instead its advancement or evolution.

Democratic conservatism is not an elite, top-down, or hierarchical conservatism, where the interests of the few are paraded as the causes of the many, but rather a popular or populist conservatism where the flow is equally from the bottom up. Democratic conservatism is about one dimension of the new partnership between the people and those who represent and serve them in government.

It is based on the concept that has been gradually emerging of Canadians as a "sovereign people." It espouses and champions the interests and needs of Canadians who live and work and study and raise families in this country, because it is a philosophy that seeks methods and processes to involve them more directly in public issues and decisions — after all, they will have to live with the consequences.

This is a conservatism that, as mentioned earlier, robustly embraces the full potential of what it means to be a democracy, and entrusts a greater role to an informed public in making decisions that affect them. It does not fear putting major constitutional amendments — be it in an entrenched Charter of Rights, or a Meech Lake Accord — directly to the people in a referendum for ratification.

It welcomes measures to ensure greater worker control and greater worker ownership participation in businesses where they are employed. It upholds the movement of shareholder democracy. It supports the concept of front-line decision-making, of participation by the consumer of health-care services, information programs, and job training activities in how those programs apply to their unique needs.

TRUST THE PEOPLE

The basic approach of democratic conservatism is to "trust the people," based on a belief in the collective wisdom of a well-informed public, and on the conviction that a healthy democracy ultimately depends on the consent of the governed.

To understand the growing possibilities of democratic conservatism, it is necessary to recognize what is happening in the evolution and decline of democratic socialism. Around the globe, there has recently been a turning away from socialism and social democracy. While notable exceptions remain, the unmistakable fact is that more voters are rejecting socialism, as its failures daily become clearer. What has been saving parties like the NDP, at least up to now, is the fact that they are *democratic* socialists. People like the democratic aspect of what the NDP stands for — its fight for the little guy, speaking up for the "ordinary Canadian," as Ed Broadbent called him, the battle for health programs — even though they may reject its socialist programs for the economy. Ordinary Canadians no longer seem to believe that the government can do it best. Ordinary Canadians don't want the state to run everything. They've had it with high taxes. They don't want to hear NDP proposals about nationalizing companies. Socialism as such is no longer in phase with Canadian needs. Democratic approaches are.

Democratic conservatism is therefore the answer, the constructive alternative, to democratic socialism.

Ahead of us now is the prospect of a new framework for Canadians who instinctively believe in a democratic system, and who share conservative values about a strong but limited role for government (steering the boat rather than rowing it), and about individual responsibility, work, family, community, and spiritual values.

Our democratic institutions in Canada are, in spite of the problems that afflict their operation, still our greatest resource for making our world what we collectively believe it ought to be, particularly if we use them to their fullest potential, and if we remain vigilant about finding ways to improve laws and modernize our procedures.

For this way of life, too many Canadians before us have struggled through the pioneering days of democracy — to win the right to vote for women and natives and other groups who found themselves the butt of racial discrimination; to curb spending so that our politics is not just a rich man's game; and to ensure balance in political programming over the public air waves. Many Canadians have also died in wars to protect us against totalitarian and militaristic states. So many have struggled and sacrificed that we can do no less today than honour them and serve ourselves by vigorously exercising our democratic rights and obligations.

Many Canadians today are questioning the gap between rhetoric and reality in our country's governmental operations. Critical thinking is more widespread in our society than ever before. While the language of our classical parliamentary arrangements continues to be used, a great many Canadians — I would now say a substantial majority — understand that the meaning has changed. Renewal is already under way. What we now await is transformation of the system into a hands-on democracy based on the trust of the people.

ABOUT THE AUTHOR
Patrick Boyer, QC, MP

A lawyer and author, Patrick Boyer was first elected to the House of Commons in the 1984 general election and re-elected in 1988, representing the Toronto-area riding of Etobicoke-Lakeshore. In April 1989 he was appointed parliamentary secretary to External Affairs Minister Joe Clark until May 1991, when he was appointed parliamentary secretary to National Defence Minister Marcel Masse. In March 1993 he was appointed parliamentary secretary to Industry, Science and Technology Minister Michael Wilson.

In private law practice before entering Parliament, Boyer was a partner in the law firm of Fraser & Beatty, specializing in communication law, corporate and commercial law, and election law, and had an extensive practice in the Western Arctic, being a member of both the Ontario and Northwest Territories Bars. On January 1, 1992, he was awarded the designation of Queen's Counsel in recognition of his contribution to Canadian law by authoring six books on election law in Canada.

His books include *Political Rights*, *Lawmaking by the People*, *Money and Message*, *Election Law in Canada*, *Local Elections in Canada*, *The People's Mandate*, *Direct Democracy*, and *Hands-on Democracy*.

Boyer has written a weekly newspaper column and contributed articles to a number of Canadian periodicals for many years. He has worked as a journalist in Saskatchewan, Ontario, and Quebec, and is a member of the Writers' Union of Canada.

He was executive director (1983-84) of the Federal Task Force on Conflict of Interest, appointed by Prime Minister Pierre Trudeau. He served as executive assistant to Ontario

Attorney General Arthur Wishart, and also worked in the office of opposition leader Robert Stanfield, responsible for housing and urban affairs, in 1969.

He is a member of the Canadian Civil Liberties Association, Amnesty International, the Churchill Society, the Canadian Institute of International Affairs, the Arctic Institute of North America, the Canadian Council on International Law, the Lions Club, and the Royal Canadian Legion.

As an active parliamentarian, Boyer has chaired committees on equality rights, the status of disabled persons, and election law reform. He has also had many private member's bills before the Commons, ranging from referendums to control of government subsidies. His bill the Centennial Flame Research Award Act for the benefit of Canadians with disabilities, became law — a rare accomplishment for a private member.

Boyer was born in 1945 at Bracebridge, Ontario, where his father, Robert Boyer, represented the Muskoka riding in the Ontario legislature for seventeen years and with Boyer's mother, Patricia Boyer, ran the local weekly newspaper, *The Herald-Gazette*.

Patrick holds an honours B.A. degree in economics and political science from Carleton University, an M.A. degree in Canadian history from the University of Toronto, and a law degree, also from the University of Toronto. He has also studied French-Canadian literature at Université de Montréal, and international law at the Academy of the International Court of Justice, The Hague.

Boyer is married to the former Corinne Mudde of the Netherlands. She was with the foreign service of the Dutch government, and in Canada has worked as an investigator in the Ombudsman's office, was with the Ontario Ministry of Justice responsible for French-language court services, and today is supporting her husband's work and is president of Artemis Enterprises and Canadian Shield Communications Corporation.